Other Titles by Edwin Page

Non-Fiction

All is Divine
Everyday Magic
Field Notes from a Compassionate Life
The Gentle Man & the Butterfly: The Complete Story (only on Kindle)
The Gentle Man & the Butterfly, Volume 1: The Light Rises
The Gentle Man & the Butterfly, Volume 2: The Darkness Falls
Twin Flames: Poetry of Love

Historical Fiction

Alabama Bake Sale
Butterfly: Part One
Butterfly: Part Two
The Hanging Tree
Oona
Pine Ridge (contemporary/supernatural/historical)
Runaway
Homestead (Runaway Series, Book Two)
Chickadee (Runaway Series, Book Three)
Providence (Runaway Series, Book Four)
Savage
Snow Dancer (sequel to Savage)
The Shack on the Hill
Tomorrow (historical/science-fiction)
Where Seagulls Fly (2013 Edition) (first of three set in Cornwall)
Song of the Sea (second of three set in Cornwall)
The Shepherd of St Just (final of three set in Cornwall)

Life After Mental Abuse

A Personal Journey

By Edwin Page

Curved Brick

First published to Kindle & paperback in 2023
by Curved Brick, UK.

No. 89

To my mother, Cheryl, Caroline, Fleurs, Sandi and Gill

thank you for your support and understanding

Life After Mental Abuse

Contents

'I wish none of this had happened.'
'So do all who live to see such times, but that is not for them to decide. All you have to decide is what to do with the time that is given to you.'

J.R.R. Tolkien, *The Fellowship of the Ring*

Introduction

There's an old proverb that goes; 'if the prey do not produce their version of the tale, the predators will always be the heroes in stories of the hunt.' Well, it's time for one of the prey to tell their story and the predators to be seen for who they really are so others may gain greater awareness.

That's what this book is; the story of my recovery from sustained mental abuse conducted by a predator. It's also so much more. It lets other victims know they're not alone. It provides insight into the effects of such abuse so those who experience it may find encouragement and ways to cope. It helps family and friends know better how to react and aid those suffering. Finally, it serves to increase awareness within the general population, not just in relation to the results of mental abuse, but also the signs and symptoms of such. In this, I hope others will avoid becoming victims and recognise when someone they know is being preyed upon.

The kinds of abuse I endured include manipulation, deceit and cruelty. The primary form I was subjected to is termed 'mixed messages,' which is most commonly associated with people who have Narcissistic Personality Disorder. It can be very subtle and insidious, yet also very powerful, not only in relation to controlling the victim, but in destabilising their mental health. This type of abuse often goes undetected. Because of these attributes, it needs to be brought out into the open. The more people that become aware of it, the more it will be spotted before it does too much damage.

Mixed messages involves such things as the abuser's actions not matching their words. Constant dramas and issues, along with regularly changing moods, mean there is always an element of unpredictability and this in turn means you can rarely settle, but are often alert to what may come next.

Essentially, if you're being mentally abused by someone who employs mixed messages, you never know what mood they'll be in when they wake, get off the phone, come in from work or even as the day progresses. You can never quite be sure where you stand, especially when they're telling you they care and yet their actions don't support this.

You never know how you'll be treated from one moment to the next, sometimes being showered with affection, sometimes receiving only silence. In fact, they can be so different from one day to the next that the victim can even feel as if the person they know has temporarily been replaced by a stranger. They promise things such as a proper response or a call later and then never deliver. They make plans for the future, ones which are in accordance with your dreams and desires, but these never materialise.

All this makes them extremely unpredictable and unreliable. It makes you increasingly careful of what you say and do just in case you cause one of the shifts. It can also make you think you're doing something wrong, whereas in truth the issue is entirely with the abuser. In turn, you begin to think about them more and more, wondering how you can help, if there's deeper issues at play, what you can do better or change in order to bring them stability.

This shift of attention to their needs is called 'extrinsic focus.' It, along with a state of confusion, is a common symptom of mixed messages and can become so intense that the victim no longer pays attention to their own needs. This is aided and abetted by the abuser not validating them. Instead, the abuser is focussed on their own life and rarely, if ever, asks about you or shows any consideration, thereby devaluing yours.

Your thoughts and actions become fixed on the abuser and the situation. You try to puzzle out all the changes and what can be done to improve things. You put every effort into making their life as good as possible in order to bring them, and you, stability. In this, the abuser achieves their goal; a person totally dedicated to their wellbeing and willing to bend over backwards to please them.

The victim and those in their life are often totally unaware of what's happening until it's too late, until extrinsic focus has been achieved and the abused simply can't stop thinking about their abuser, often utterly confused by what's happening. Something else which commonly goes unseen is that the changeable and unpredictable conditions have nothing whatsoever to do with the abused. They are manufactured by the abuser in order to destabilise the victim which, along with extrinsic focus, makes them much more susceptible to being controlled.

As you can see, mixed messages can be a very effective tool when it comes to manipulation. It allows the abuser to exert a great deal of control without ever appearing to do anything untoward. Everything seems relatively innocent to all but the most perceptive observer. This, along with the extent of the damage it can do, makes it extremely dangerous and the more people who become aware of it, the better.

As well as intense confusion and extrinsic focus, I suffered from other symptoms caused by the abuse in general. These included paranoia, fear, withdrawal and a lack of motivation to carry out even the most basic everyday tasks, like opening the post. I was barely able to function and consistently overcome by waves of sadness, devastation, frustration, inactivity and more confusion. To say it was a struggle in the early weeks and months is far beyond an understatement.

Most of these symptoms were present before the relationship in question came to an end. They dovetail its final months and the beginning of recovery, which actually came some time after contact had ended because I was still uncovering the truth about my abuser's activities.

I was surprised by how many people treated the end of my abusive relationship as if it was the end of a normal relationship. This isn't the case due to important psychological differences. Abusers often target weaknesses and purposefully destabilise the mentality of the person they're abusing. They can be intentionally confusing and unkind. The mental impact of an abusive relationship runs deep, whether that relationship is with a family member, friend, colleague or life partner.

My abuser falls into the latter category. She is someone I continue to care about and who remains the love of my life. How could this be the case after she mentally abused me? Like physical abuse, mental abuse is not constant. This means it's still possible to share beautiful and amazing times with your abuser, to enjoy smiles and laughter in their company, and to love them deeply. In my case, these good times far outweighed the abuse, at least while we were living together. This also means that, to those outside the relationship, it can seem all but perfect.

When it comes to my close friends, I've always been very open about my life and so some became aware that something was amiss. Both early in the relationship and in the final year and a half, friends warned me that I was being subjected to mental abuse and even pointed out when I was being manipulated. This was often conducted in a way sometimes termed 'bread-crumbing,' my abuser using an act of kindness, a promise of good things to come, or some other carrot to keep me focussed on her. I ignored the signs that I could see, thinking they were merely a result of mental health issues my abuser claimed to have. However, I was completely blind to others until after our contact came to an end.

When it did and when I started to realise the truth, I felt worthless, lost and utterly broken. I questioned who I was and where I was going. I felt isolated and different, like there was no place for me in this world. There was a huge amount of self-doubt. I felt so ugly that I couldn't mix with other people. The good qualities on the inside seemed to count for little, had been abused and had allowed me to be taken advantage of for years. What I'd thought of as my most positive attributes had turned out to be my Achilles heal. How could I recover from all this and more? How could I heal? I didn't know but, I assure you, healing happens.

Recovery isn't easy. Sometimes it can feel all but impossible. The anguish can be so great that you can't see any way forward. You want to be able to take time out, find release from the turmoil. I'd walk around in agitation, feel like curling up in some dark corner, shed countless tears and try to sleep just to escape the impossibility of staying awake with the pain. I wanted to cry out, 'ENOUGH!' in the hope it would release some of the pressure. I didn't want to be here any more, couldn't see the point, especially if I was going to have to live with so much trauma. What I couldn't see is that even those times were part of the healing which was starting to take place.

I hope reading this book can become part of your healing if you've suffered from mental abuse. I know it can feel like you have no voice and maybe this can go some way to making you feel that you do. There can also be a sense of not being understood and of injustice as your abuser continues with their life as if nothing has happened or, worse still, as if you were the predator. There's little or no recourse to law despite the seriousness of the offence against your person, against the very essence of who you are mentally and emotionally. Maybe it can help knowing that there are others who understand, for the truth of the matter is that you are not alone, my friend.

Some people said to block her and move on. Others said they knew what I was going through. Though well intentioned, neither was realistic, helpful or showed any understanding of mentally abusive relationships. However, both provided motivation in regards writing this book in order to increase awareness of the nature and impact of such relationships. Because of this, I hope many people who haven't suffered in this way read this work. By doing so, they can be of genuine help should someone they know ever be subjected to such abuse and will have a greater chance of recognising if someone tries to abuse them, especially with the use of mixed messages.

The chapters ahead and the book itself are relatively short. This is intentional because, at the peak of my trauma, there's absolutely no way I could have faced reading a large volume. I would have retreated from that challenge, just like I retreated from so much else. Now that retreat has turned into forward motion and I know the same will happen for you.

In fact, that forward motion is soon going to happen as we move onto the opening chapter. It provides a brief account of the relationship in question and of my abuser in order to give context to the rest of the book. Chapters Two through Seven are primarily concerned with the dual impact of the abuse and the end of the relationship. They can each be viewed like layers of a picture and when they're brought together create the complete image of those early times. Chapters Eight to Fifteen chart the process of healing and recovery to date. Finally, Chapter Sixteen brings the main body of this book to its conclusion with a view to the future. I hope each contains something of use, note or interest.

Chapter One

Looking Back

Before I can talk about the recovery process, I need to briefly let you know what happened, what I was actually recovering from. This chapter outlines the events of the preceding four years and more. It also gives you an idea of my abuser's characteristics and behaviour. It is the longest in the book for these reasons, but I promise the chapters get shorter after this.

On 27th July 2018, a mutual friend introduced me to Lissa (pronounced in the same way as if spelt with one 's'). Despite being considerably younger than me, we soon became a couple and, not long afterwards, she moved into my cottage in the county of Cornwall, located in the far southwest of England. Our relationship as partners lasted for nearly three years, during which time we were engaged for 17 months after I asked her to marry me on my 47th birthday in August 2019.

We broke up early in July 2021 due to an apparent change in her sexuality. Because no one was at fault and we supposedly continued to love each other, we remained close for over a year beyond that point.

Soon after our break-up, we became what we termed 'best-friend soulmates.' Because we had such a strong connection and fulfilled all of each other's needs other than on a sexual front, Lissa put forward the suggestion that we cohabit in Sweden five to ten years in the future. For the following ten months or so, she consistently added to this plan, even purchasing books on elements of Swedish culture.

I placed my cottage on the market for her and us, stating it was my first step towards the Swedish plan and showed my commitment to our future. Lissa undertook an ecological Masters degree in Belfast, stating that it was her commitment to the same and that once it was done she'd move to mainland Europe, that nothing could keep her in the U.K.

When the Masters commenced in September 2021, we were on the phone most days for an average of around 12 hours. She'd be engaged in coursework and I'd be writing and then we'd spend the evenings chatting and watching films. At the same time, I took my cottage off the market due to a number of issues.

That was the story of the first and second semester, but the third saw me putting the cottage up for sale once again and quickly receiving an offer which was accepted. It also found Lissa undertaking a three month work placement on a small Greek island in the Aegean Sea. It was there that her treatment of me began to rapidly decline for no apparent reason.

Much of her abuse prior to that point had been covert and I was totally unaware it had taken place. Though friends and family members were already aware of some elements of her abusive behaviour and had been for quite some time, I was oblivious or choosing to ignore and disbelieve. However, it became increasingly overt and I started to notice deliberate cruelty and hurtfulness.

This change began in May 2022 and my mental health declined in response. In the final few months of our contact, she targeted my self-esteem and tore apart elements of the friendship which she knew were precious to me. Her treatment of me became increasingly unpleasant and it may be she was trying to get me to walk away so that she wouldn't appear to be the 'bad guy.'

Lissa creates the impression of someone who's a victim of mistreatment by her parents, past partners, friends and work colleagues. One of the results of this is supposed abandonment issues. This would mean that pushing me to the point when I'd have to go would allow her to claim I was just another in a long line of people who'd abandoned her.

In truth and with hindsight, the idea that she has genuine abandonment issues is unlikely. I saw many friends come and go during our four years and it was always Lissa who walked away. The fact it was 'many' serves to highlight that she's unable to maintain stable close relationships. This is one of the symptoms which point to the possibility she has a serious personality disorder. Others include pathological lying, emotional detachment, blame transference and a lack of moral boundaries.

By early August 2022, I'd secured a property on the southwest coast of Scotland. I'd come to realise she'd changed her mind about leaving the U.K. and was going to remain in Belfast after the Masters was completed. My new location would mean I'd only be a few hours travel from her and we'd be able to spend time with each other far more easily. However, I also came to suspect our friendship may not last much longer as her treatment of me remained predominantly cold and uncaring.

I was taken by the urge to write our story. At the time, I felt the love we'd shared as a couple was special and as best friends we'd enjoyed a unique experience of phone cohabitation during her first two semesters in Belfast. I thought our story was beautiful and came up with the title *The Gentle Man and the Butterfly*, deciding to couch the true story in the fiction of an older version of myself telling his nurse about the love of his life.

My 50th birthday came in late August and Lissa was particularly cruel and heartless. I came close to taking my own life because of the accumulative effect of her treatment and what was happening. The thought of committing suicide was common by that point, but that was the closest I ever came despite the abuse becoming increasingly sadistic, Lissa finding amusement in some of the hurtful things she said and did.

At the end of my birthday week, someone at one of my local pubs drunkenly told me she hadn't treated me well when working at a local branch of a nationwide hardware store and had been seeing other men. I told him in no uncertain terms that he was mistaken and didn't believe him for an instant.

A couple of weeks or so later, I mentioned what had been said to Lissa during one of our phone conversations. Her reaction wasn't what I'd expected. Instead of being horrified and checking I didn't believe it, she laughed it off. I was struck by the unexpectedness of her response.

A few days later, unable to shake a niggling feeling that something was amiss and with only hours until contracts were due to exchange on the sale of my cottage, I found the courage to text the man I'd been led to believe was her best friend at the hardware store. His reply came shortly after the exchange and I was legally bound to sell the house, I was also in an absolute state of shock after reading his response. It turned out he'd been far more than just a friend and the truth of how she'd been behaving and who she really was started to become apparent.

I came to discover she'd been sexually intimate with a number of other men during our time as a couple, including at the start of our relationship. During her employment at the hardware store, she'd told her work colleagues I was the landlord she hated, both dating and seeing men who worked there while we were engaged. It's also likely that I was her landlord when it came to the majority of the other people in her life, including her parents.

When I found out about the double life, Lissa wasn't concerned with how I felt, but about me contacting her parents. She wasn't worried about the emotional impact of her lies about them or feeling guilty she'd acted in such a way, she was simply anxious about being caught out.

I forgave everything that had been revealed at the time and said I wanted to remain in her life, to help her change and heal, believing her actions were the result of past trauma. Lissa claimed she wanted that too and was even apparently overcome by emotion during one of our calls as she talked about me being by her side while she dealt with her issues.

Only days later and after four years of daily communication in person or over the phone, she cut contact on the 22nd September 2022, using her mental health as an excuse, as she had on previous occasions. The real reason was she'd begun a new relationship and could no longer hide it from me or maintain our degree of contact. Neither could she easily hide me from her new partner.

Further, she likely didn't want someone in her life who was starting to see who she really is. She needs everyone around her to be convinced of the persona she fabricates, partly so she can convince herself it's real, something helped by her use of blame transference and emotional detachment. Essentially, Lissa lies to herself as well as everyone else and my presence only served to highlight this.

Due to me contacting a couple of her past friends in order to discover the truth about some of the things she'd told me, she renewed contact on 11th October. It was the day that the sale of the cottage completed. What's more, I'd driven for six and a half hours through the night to temporarily move in with my mother until the purchase of the Scottish property completed, the majority of my possessions put into storage.

Lissa was annoyed I'd tried to contact other people, at least one of them having got in touch to tell her. Rather than confronting the issue directly, she created a charade, pretending I'd done so in order to find out if she was okay, something I'd not even touched upon when tracking down the people in question. She tried to find out if I'd contacted anyone else and told me to message her directly if I wanted to check on her wellbeing. She was essentially trying to keep track of my activities and, during the three and a half hour conversation, barely mentioned the move.

That was one of our final three calls, all of which happened that same week. The last was on Thursday 13th. In it, she brought the last remnants of what we'd shared to an end, including claiming that Sweden had only ever been a dream. She even expressed annoyance in regards me telling the people I'd contacted that we'd been engaged, stating she told people we'd been best friends who lived together. By the end of the call, I was reeling. I was also left with only the vague promise of having a couple of calls a week, which I suspect were more to keep tabs on me rather than out of any real desire to keep me in her life.

She then went to visit her eldest brother and his family in California and I set to work on the story of what I'd once thought was 'our' love. Despite having considerable evidence to support everything that had happened, I changed her name to Lucy. I wanted to protect her, as I'd tried to do throughout our time together due to her appearance of helplessness and vulnerability, along with my love for her. I was still convinced she was the person

I'd believed her to be and the dark side I'd uncovered was just that; a side of her, like a shadow, a separate entity.

The fact I'm using Lissa's real first name now shows how far I've come, how much I've accepted and healed. I see that others need protecting from her, that the darkness *is* her and much of the light is simply the persona she projects. She is willing to damage people's mental and emotional health for her own ends, which means she's a threat to the wellbeing of others. She's also prepared to let them potentially ruin their lives due to her influence, as can be seen in relation to the sale of my cottage.

Lissa had around ten months from when I first proposed selling it to the exchange of contracts, ten months in which to reveal what she truly thought about cohabiting in Sweden. She could have also come clean about her conduct when we were a couple so that my decision could be made in full knowledge of the truth. If she wanted to maintain her secrets and deceptions, she could have simply walked away in order that I didn't sell up. Instead, she continued to maintain and build upon the idea of a Swedish life together and never told me even one element of what I came to discover.

When I ask myself why, all I can think of is that she still thought I may come in useful if things didn't work out after the Masters. I know she operates from a self-serving perspective and this is likely how she viewed the situation; in light of how it could benefit her and without thought for its impact upon me.

Also in relation to using her real first name, it has to be noted that she made the choices to act the way she did. These choices defined the content of *The Gentle Man and the Butterfly* and this book, and she should be able to face the consequences of her actions.

As I wrote our story, I stumbled across an article called 'Narcissists Mixed Messages' on a site called Psych

Central (which is included in Appendix II). It not only explained much of her behaviour in the early months of our relationship and in the year and a half since she'd moved out of the cottage, but also during our entire time together. Further, it also explained my declining mental health in the last few months when her abusive treatment became less subtle and more open.

While she was in America visiting her brother, I came to realise I had to say 'goodbye' out of self-preservation. This I did via Whatsapp upon her return to the U.K. and, a week later, she responded. There was no apology or affection. If I'm any guess, there was also little truth to what she expressed in relation to seeking genuine help, something she'd admitted she'd never done in the past, always lying to her therapists.

In the days that followed her goodbye, I discovered more about her behaviour which she'd kept hidden. This was thanks to continuing writing *The Gentle Man and the Butterfly*. These revelations included that she'd consistently lied throughout the four years, manipulating and using me in a way which is often termed 'gaslighting.' Her change in sexual orientation and all the angst she'd expressed in relation to it was a deceit. At the same time as claiming her sex drive had turned off and to be struggling with her sexuality, Lissa had been having a relationship with the man I'd thought was her closest friend at the hardware store.

One of the discoveries which had the greatest impact related to when she'd moved out of the cottage to take new employment near her parents in Herefordshire, staying with them during that time. This had occurred at the end of February 2021, when we were still a couple, and turned out to be a complete fabrication. She had in fact moved somewhere nearby in Cornwall and remained at the hardware store, lying every single day for almost four months about her supposed duties at the new job and life at her parents' house.

That's the story of mine and Lissa's time together in very broad strokes. There's so much more to it than that. This includes little things, like Lissa saying she'd been rewarded with my friendship after coming out as gay because she'd been so open and honest, to the big things, like Lissa sending a video of her and four friends giving me the finger while on the Greek island and claiming it related to the organisation they were working for. If you want to read it all, you'll find it in *The Gentle Man and the Butterfly*, which is available as two volumes entitled *The Light Rises* and *The Darkness Falls* in Kindle and paperback formats or as a Kindle exclusive edition subtitled *The Complete Story*.

There's something which wasn't mentioned in the story that may be useful to some. In the two and a half weeks between her initially cutting contact and me having to move out of my cottage, I placed numerous statements about her and our time together around the interior. I'd expressed that I'd never turn my back on Lissa to a neighbour with experience of mental health issues. She told me Lissa was likely to renew contact and advised me that in the meantime I should focus on the negatives in order to maintain boundaries when that happened.

Taking sheets of printing paper and a marker pen, I proceeded to write over 60 statements in large lettering, of which around thirty were then tacked around my house. These included such things as 'Lissa is toxic,' 'you've had a lucky escape' and 'she is a liar.' These served as reminders, especially as the realities of what she'd done and who she is were so far removed from the image she presents. This activity was omitted from our story purely because it could have undermined the first of what turned out to be three endings. I mention it here as it may be helpful for others to do similar in order to begin the process of moving on.

I still believe there's some light in Lissa, that she's capable of genuine kindness, warmth, affection and empathy. However, like the sun and moon tattoo on her side, I think the light is being eclipsed by the darkness. With each manipulation, each lie, each cruelty, she undermines her own self-image and the darkness grows.

Maybe it's naïve, but I also still believe she can change, but she has to recognise the need and be totally committed to such. She would also need the support of someone who knows the truth of who she is and likely have to live with them, otherwise she'd simply be tempted back into previous behavioural patterns. She cannot be trusted, even by herself, to do it alone.

Because of my continued compassion for Lissa, I hope she will one day be free of her abusive traits. Then she'll be able to maintain lasting relationships containing affection and love which haven't been artificially manufactured. Moreover, she'll be able to love in return and thereby find a sense of fulfilment I believe she's yet to experience.

Though I'd born the brunt of her abuse because of our closeness and other circumstances, I came to realise I hadn't been singled out for special treatment. She lives double lives with, lies to and manipulates everyone in her life. This is largely thanks to the creation of a false persona which makes it seem like she couldn't possibly behave in such ways. In order to create her persona, Lissa employs a number of strategies.

One is to present an air of neediness, coupled with a degree of helplessness. Both inspire compassion and care in others. This is especially the case as she emphasises mental health issues she supposedly has, such as anxiety. I say 'supposedly' because her actions revealed her anxiety to be minimal and likely connected with the web of lies and deceptions she chooses to weave.

Another strategy is to highlight criticisms and unkind behaviour on the part of her mother. As with the anxiety, it's likely these are either half-truths or fabrications intended to create further sympathy. They help form the image of someone being treated unfairly by the very person she should be able to rely on the most.

Lissa also says things like 'you know how empathic I am' or 'you know how soft-hearted I can be.' Because these are statements, they encourage you to believe them, even when there is little or no evidence in relation to her actual behaviour. She is *telling* you that you know these things so why would you question them? It's a clever device and, in relation to the example statements, had me believing both were true. With hindsight, I find little sign of either during the four years and more I knew her.

Early in the relationship, she made it abundantly clear she wouldn't tolerate any degree of lying or cheating, something most people wouldn't do as it's self-evident. This was another device, one intended to create the impression of someone who found such behaviour morally reprehensible. In turn, I was more likely to trust her, even when situations arose which contained the distinct possibility of misbehaviour on her part.

Adding to the idea that Lissa is trustworthy is the impression she creates of being a victim. You'd never suspect a victim of bad conduct or being an abuser and she so does everything she can to maintain this image. Due to this, she may well be what's known as a 'vulnerable' narcissist.

In this light, the proverb that began the *Introduction* needs a little tinkering. Lissa doesn't cast herself as the hero of the hunt, but instead portrays herself as its victim. She is a predator pretending to be prey. This means the people in her life remain unaware of what's really happened.

This role reversal when telling her stories of the hunt shows a great deal of deceitfulness and manipulation. It's also a means by which she transfers blame to the other person involved. I experienced this firsthand in a number of ways.

Firstly, there was the ex from when she was studying for her bachelor's degree before I knew her. According to Lissa, he'd spread lies about her amongst their friends and also had a meltdown at the annex in which she lived prior to moving in with me, smashing things and ranting while high on cocaine. She was clearly casting herself in the role of victim and claiming he was the predator. In hindsight, I think it likely he discovered her lies and revealed them to their friends and his 'meltdown' may well have been related to his frustration at her behaviour.

When briefly communicating with the man she'd been seeing at the hardware store, he told me they'd been together for six to seven months. He also said she'd been dating another man who worked there before going out with him and had sent naked shots from my cottage. Lissa denied these things and insisted he was lashing out because his ego had been damaged, stating categorically that he was lying and she was innocent. This put her in the role of victim and cast him as the predator. Everything he'd stated turned out to be true.

When it came to an ex who was a married man, she also cast him in the role of predator, saying he'd preyed on her because of her mental health issues. The same allegation was made in regards at least one other man and I suspect that in both instances she was far from the victim she claimed to be.

I also suspect that I was cast in this predatory role while she was on the Greek island, which is why I received the video of Lissa and her friends giving me the finger. Once again, she'd swapped the roles to suit her purpose and maintain her disguise, remaining a wolf amidst the unsuspecting flock.

The above are just some of the ways she maintains the persona of someone meek, mild, vulnerable, harmless and kind. She also maintains a degree of childishness when interacting with her parents and often employs the use of a soft voice. As with lying and living double lives, this persona is presented to everyone in her life. Any challenge to it is greeted with irritation and anger. She will fight to preserve both it and the deceits which hide the truth of her aggressive personality and the possible presence of a serious personality disorder.

I experienced this on at least two occasions and know how forceful she can be when trying to defend the web of illusion surrounding the reality of who she is. This, as mentioned, is probably because Lissa also needs to believe the illusion. She is likely hiding from herself as much as she's hiding herself from everyone else. She knows who she really is, but won't face it, which means she'll never deal with her issues.

The persona is essentially sheep's clothing for the wolf. It allows her to blend in without most people suspecting the truth which is being concealed. This returns us to the proverb at the start of the book once again. It was sent to me by a friend after she'd read *The Gentle Man and the Butterfly* and she informed me that the latter stages of mine and Lissa's story had brought it to mind. This resonates with a feeling I had when writing about that part of our time together; that it was like a cat toying with a mouse.

People with tendencies like hers do not like to be called out and hate their bubble of falsehoods being threatened. Maybe that's because they realise a single pin can cause it to pop, as it did with Lissa. That pin was the response I received from her work colleague and friend. The 'pop' may well have been all but immediate, but accepting the reality of what it revealed was not. It takes time to adjust to such a huge reality shift. It's something I'm still doing, but a clear understanding of who the person really is does slowly emerge as the remnants of their bubble disappear due to lack of substance. The dust settles and they are hidden no more.

I was initially unable to accept I'd been mentally abused, was still trying to come to terms with the clash between the person I thought I knew and the reality of who Lissa really is. This slowly changed and, in turn, I had to accept she'd been my abuser. This was especially hard because I continued to look back at our time together with fondness, to have great affection for her and regard her as the love of my life.

However, it became plain to see that she'd been playing games, not just with me, but with others in her life. She would hint at the truth behind her lies through such things as comments or photos. It was as if she enjoyed the excitement created by the additional risk of discovery. Such behaviour underlined her ability to be cold and calculating, along with the enjoyment of creating confusion and pain. It also serves to underline her impaired conscience or lack of one, along with her lack of moral boundaries.

There's nothing she won't use to manipulate situations in accordance with her wishes and to get the attention she craves. She uses her mind and body. She uses her family, her mental health and, in my case, even used her sexual orientation. She consistently manufactures praise and attention. She also wants those closest to her to be proud of her, failing to see she's ultimately got to be proud of herself. This and more is clear to see with hindsight but, trust me, it was invisible for the vast majority of the time she was in my life.

Now, the silt has cleared from my eyes and I can see the truth with increased clarity. This was helped by re-editing *The Gentle Man and the Butterfly* during the course of writing this book, months after its initial release. I hadn't been able to face it back then but, as I read what I'd written and thanks to the time which had elapsed since first doing so, I was able to see the truth of who she was and how badly she'd treated me, especially at the start and end of our time together.

Seeing the situation for what it was is an important step in healing. Until you can, you are not facing the realities of what has happened to you, and that was the case with me for quite some time. This was largely out of the love I still feel for Lissa and the hope she would return. It was a false hope, and I needed to recognise that too. Such things and more will be discussed in the coming chapters, but there was still a long way for me to go before I reached those milestones, as you'll now see…

Chapter Two

Moving Yet Static

There are a number of reasons moving out may be necessary after the end of an abusive relationship. These include the property having to be sold due to joint ownership, financial pressures of a single income or to escape the memories of the past. As you've just read, I had voluntarily sold my cottage in order to move closer to Lissa and as a step towards our proposed future together.

Though both reasons were made null and void by the termination of our contact, there was little choice but to continue along the path which would lead me to the southwest coast of Scotland and so, after a stay of just over three months at my mother's, I finally moved to my new house on 19th January 2023. Arriving after another all-night drive, I set to the business of making it a home once the removal men had been and gone, my two cats familiarising themselves with the interior while I set things up.

There were no tears and I was glad to find that I really liked the property, especially the sea views. There was also a sense of there being no other viable choices open to me. This wasn't defeatist, it was simply accepting that, for the time being at least, this would be my home and my life. It was down to me to make the best or worst of it.

I unpacked most of my things over the course of the first few days and placed the few items of furniture I owned where I wanted them. Once finished, I was struck by a realisation; I'd done so with Lissa in mind without even knowing it.

Two seats rested before the front windows with a coffee table between, two seats which were meant to be occupied by us. A drinks cabinet had been set up in a corner of the dining room, one which was there for us to pour ourselves shots as we got tipsy and music played. Two small UV lights had been placed on top of the DVD shelves in the lounge to be turned on when we danced around on drunken nights filled with smiles and laughter.

When I realised what I'd done, I broke down. I ached for her to be there, for her to occupy the other seat in the window across from me and to be pouring drinks with her in the kitchen-diner. We'd shared so many good times and I wanted to share more despite all I'd found out. At this early stage, the true nature of who she was and what she'd done hadn't sank in and I was still yearning for a return to some semblance of what I thought we'd had.

I also put a few things on display fully aware their placement was motivated by my continuing love of Lissa and wish for her return. A framed image of us as angels in a moonlit clearing that I'd created via Photoshop was placed on a shelf in my bedroom, the two of us having posed naked for the photograph during Lissa's final ever visit to Cornwall early in August 2021. Beside it was a soft toy of Jiminy Cricket I'd discovered in a charity shop while staying with my mother. This represented Lissa's love of Disney. Moreover, it was linked to an emotional response she'd had at the thought of me being by her side as she dealt with her mental health issues. She'd told me I'd be like her Jiminy Cricket, her conscience. A few days later, she cut contact.

I placed a heart-shaped stone of white quartz that I'd found on a beach when out on one of our walks in front of the picture. On top of it was set an engagement ring she'd bought for me in September 2020, which was pewter with a copper heart.

I admitted the first two of these things had been placed on display to friends and family, but didn't mention the ring to most. When it came to the Photoshop image, I used the excuse that it wasn't of any particular occasion and that each time I looked at it I sent her healing and love. This was true, but it was also there because I hoped we'd be together again one day. It symbolised that wish. It also symbolised my belief she could heal; both our wings pure white. As for Jiminy, everyone close to me knew what she'd said in relation to him, and so little explanation was needed. However, I did come to realise her comments about me being her Jiminy, her conscience, revealed she was probably aware she hadn't got one or that hers was impaired.

Placing those items was evidence of a continuing hope that Lissa would visit or even come to live with me in Scotland, though I didn't dare put voice to this with my friends or family as I knew what their reaction would be to such a revelation. I bought outdoor fairy lights and strung them outside the patio doors of the dining area to make the house feel magical for her.

I also bought a large metal butterfly and a butterfly wind rocker, the first being hung on the wall above the angel picture and the second placed in the back garden. Both were purchased with her in mind.

Butterflies had been a common theme during our time as a couple and especially when we were supposedly best friends, one of our pet names for each other at that time being 'butterfly soulmates.' This was partly due to the Disney film *Encanto*, which had been 'our' film as best friends (*The Greatest Showman* having been 'our' film as a couple). One of the symbols used in *Encanto* is butterflies, which express the idea of kindred spirits having to fly their separate ways in order to one day be reunited. Deep inside, that's how I viewed the time at hand; a time of separation which wouldn't last.

I'd placed magnetic butterflies on every radiator in the house and noticed I'd predominantly put them in pairs without even realising it; the symbolism being of Lissa and I dancing through life together. I also bought two dishes featuring pairs of butterflies to compliment the butterfly plates I already owned.

It's clear that in those early days and weeks, she was woven into my thoughts and actions. I'd moved, but my feelings had remained static. I'd yet to accept the realities of what had happened and it may be I was still in shock after the revelations which came at and after the end of our contact.

Something which soon became habitual was a weekly call with Caroline (called Sarah in *The Gentle Man and the Butterfly*). These took place every Sunday evening and continue to this day. I commonly pace when having a long phone conversation, the only exception to date being when I used to speak with Lissa.

During one of the earlier calls, I found myself in the kitchen. Looking down its length to the dining area, I was overcome with the sense that the house was waiting to be filled with life, could almost see people at the dining table. The feeling was so strong that I excitedly told her about it.

It arose again when I next spoke to Sandi (who was the only person to retain her real name in the story of mine and Lissa's time together). I told her about it too, once more filled with a sense of happiness to come.

It was a few weeks later when the root of the feeling made itself apparent. I was in the kitchen and saw what I'd previously only sensed, like a vision of sorts. Lissa and I were preparing food in the galley kitchen. Our two children were seated on the far side of the table in the dining area at the far end, full of beans and eager to eat. The kitchen-diner was filled with a sense of happy family life. I became distraught in response, knowing it was likely behind my previous feelings when speaking with Caroline and Sandi. Filled with great sadness, I knew the vision was an echo of all the hopes and dreams I'd once had for our future together.

Many of those hopes and dreams had been expressed in *The Gentle Man and the Butterfly* and writing our story had been like continuing the daily contact we'd had during the four years. This meant that, for the majority of my time at my mother's, I'd still felt like Lissa was in my life.

This came to an end with the move to Scotland. In turn, my sense of isolation and difference which her presence had once silenced was felt more keenly than ever before. She was the first person whose presence had caused those feelings to fall quiet and this helped give rise to a sense of fulfilment when I was with her. Without her, the silence of those feelings was over and they returned with a roar. I felt like no one understood me and like there was no one to talk to about all the things which we'd once spoken about. This ranged from the relatively mundane, like movies, to the more profound, like the fact we should have greater compassion for all life because each living being is both individual and unique.

My new location anchored my internal sense of isolation in physical reality. Lissa had described western Cornwall as 'the arse end of nowhere,' saying it was too remote and that she was pleased I was moving. However, the cottage in Scotland was far more remote and the area less populated. Local amenities were sparse, the nearest store being in the next village and the nearest supermarket an hour away, whereas the village store had been across the road in Cornwall and the nearest supermarket only ten minutes away. More importantly, hundred of miles now separated me from the majority of my friends and family.

This physical isolation accentuated my mental and emotional isolation. I felt totally and utterly alone. The only way I could have a conversation was by ringing someone, and that's never the same as being in their company. At that time, I found myself calling my mother almost daily, partly because I'd just spent over three months with her and partly because she was free far more often then my friends, most of whom had jobs.

The time of year also didn't help; the days still short and the nights long. It was too cold to be out in the garden and this also discouraged me from going for walks. It took a couple of weeks or so until I finally did so for the first time, going to the nearby beach and finding myself wandering alone along its sand and shingle. I took a few photos and picked up driftwood, but found no joy in the activity.

In that time, the house was my 'safe place,' and remains so to this day, but in a more usual way. The doors were kept locked and I stayed away from the world. Behind those doors, there was one positive I was aware of; I'd escaped the memories that would have surrounded me in Cornwall. In Scotland there were only thoughts and imaginings of Lissa being there, but nothing more solid, and that was a small mercy.

If I'd have remained in the cottage where we'd lived together for two and a half years, I believe I'd have languished far longer than has turned out to be the case. Of our time together there, by far the lion's share of the memories were good ones. This is altering with time as what she was doing 'behind the scenes' continues to sink in, along with the reality of her purposefully positioning herself as a victim in order to become central to both the relationship and my focus, and the continual mental abuse through mixed messages.

Because of this lack of memories, the house felt free of the past. This and the time of year meant I managed very few walks, my lack of motivation and energy meaning I barely left the three-seater settee unless it was to visit the bathroom or have a coffee and smoke some of my toothpick-style roll-ups.

When I did go for a walk, I'd look to the driveway with both apprehension and expectancy when returning along the quiet country road. I was trying to discern if Lissa's car was there and, on one particular walk which took me over a nearby coastal headland affording continued views of the house, I kept looking back for the same reason. On the return, my eyes barely left the cottage and were drawn to every one of the few vehicles that passed by to see if she was approaching. The idea that she would just turn up wouldn't leave me and this draws us onto the next layer of what life was like during those early weeks in Scotland…

Chapter Three

Fear & Paranoia

For the first three weeks in my new home, I carried a knife in my pocket. A shocking statement, but true nonetheless. It goes to show what an impact abuse can have and how the abuser can be viewed once ties have been cut.

I'd stumbled across the lock-knife while unpacking. Though it was initially placed in a drawer, it was soon taken back out and tucked in my pocket. Why? To give me a sense of security and means to defend myself. I was fearful that Lissa would find out about the books and turn up unannounced in order to attack me, possibly both verbally and physically. I'd seen her exhibit bursts of aggressive and often indignant anger, not towards me, but most commonly in relation to her immediate family. As I stated in Chapter One, I'd also experienced the vehement way in which she defends her deceits and the persona she presents to the world. Publishing our story had revealed both and more to anyone who cared to read it and I knew she'd likely be infuriated by this.

So concerned was I for my safety that I'd given instructions to my mother before leaving, telling her to make sure Lissa's family knew what had really happened if something befell me in Scotland. This didn't just relate to the possibility of Lissa harming me, but also to continued thoughts of suicide, though I never mentioned the latter for obvious reasons.

I'd also bought an external hard drive onto which the manuscripts and all the evidence supporting them was saved. This was left at my mother's just in case Lissa tried to burn down my new home in order to try and be rid of the proof, not just of how she'd behaved, but of things like our engagement, of which her family and friends were completely unaware.

Despite this, there was also part of me that hoped she'd see the deep love and compassion evident in my words when her anger faded. I thought that somehow, just maybe, reading what I'd written could break through to the goodness I still believed she possessed and she'd realise not only that she needed to change, but also that she loved me.

It was a strange contrast of feelings, one brought on by the clash of Lissa's persona with the reality of who she is and the clash of the relationship I thought we'd had with the truth that she hadn't regarded it or me in the way I'd been led to believe. Both my hopes and my fear of attack were unrealistic but, from the place I was in and in light of previous behaviour on her part, they were perfectly logical.

These thoughts and reactions were only to be expected after sustained mental abuse and because of how I continued to feel about her. In regards the latter, I still hadn't come to see her in a realistic light, but clung onto the idea that her darkness was merely a side of her, believing her light could win out, especially with my support. In regards to the former, any kind of abuse is an assault, whether physically or mentally. You are under attack and, when it comes to mental abuse, this attack can go undetected. It's like being repeatedly clawed as the abuser distracts you with words and deeds to keep you believing they're really a sheep. The blood slowly drains from your life and you fade, becoming increasingly focussed on them and their life, their control increasing as a result. You don't realise what's happening, but you sense a change in you and sometimes see clues as to the other person's true identity, the wolf's disguise briefly slipping and allowing you to see what sharp teeth they have.

As the effects of the continuing abuse increase over time, they become more obvious and other people may notice. They may also point out untoward behaviour on the part of the other person or start to realise what's happening. It could be that circumstances reveal the wounds being inflicted or the fleece is removed by the wolf in question, at least in part. To mix my metaphors, this is ground zero; the point of impact, one which will explode your life and bring everything you thought you knew into question in a whirlwind of confusion.

When it comes to my experience, the truth about Lissa's intentions and activities during the four years she'd been in my life was revealed in all three ways described in the preceding paragraph. The latter two brought with them a delayed sense of danger and devastation. This was intensified by the suddenness and unexpectedness of the revelations. The act of carrying the knife was evidence of this sense of danger and bore testament to the amount of damage Lissa had inflicted. I'd got to the point when I felt totally insecure, the threat of continued assault lurking around every corner.

It wasn't until a few weeks later, during a Sunday evening call with Caroline, that I finally admitted to carrying the knife. Just putting voice to the fact helped me see it was unnecessary. I'd moved on since first placing it in my pocket and realised the act of doing so simply perpetuated my fear. If I could release the knife, put it back in the drawer, I would also be releasing some of the hold the fear had over me. Knowing this caused me to put it away while Caroline and I were on the phone, and I never felt the need for it again.

That's the most striking example of the fear I felt as a result of the abuse, but there were others. The most subtle was the sense of agitation at the thought of hearing from her. I'd become anxious, restless and sweaty. My stomach would feel light as I anticipated the sound of my phone announcing a call or message.

When she'd been in my life, that reaction had been common in the last four months or so. With hindsight, I can see it was related to not knowing which Lissa I'd discover on the other end; the Lissa who appeared to be loving, thoughtful and affectionate or the Lissa who was unkind, cold and sometimes cruel.

When at my mother's, my agitation in relation to hearing from her was very strong towards the end of December. The first volume of our story was due for release on the 1st January and the closer that date came the more intense my feelings of unease became. I was nervous of Lissa's response to the books.

Despite changing the names of those mentioned, omitting numerous locations and giving very few clues as to people's appearance, I made the decision to publish the books under 'anonymous.' I claimed this was to further protect identities, but it was really out of fear. Some friends were surprised and impressed I'd found the courage to publish the work at all, knowing full well how manipulated I'd been and how in love I still was. However, at a point when I was doubting my strength to do so, it was a simple comment made by a character in a detective series that gave me the impetus to carry on as planned.

The character was a woman who'd committed a number of murders. She was being questioned and when her husband was mentioned, she said something like, 'well, he always was a spineless man' with obvious contempt. This immediately brought to mind the way I'd heard Lissa reference me in a phone call early in our relationship and a particular photograph from shortly before she moved out, one in which her expression and gesture had communicated the same feeling with absolute certainty. I considered it likely she'd viewed me as spineless and I was also starting to view myself in the same light. Even in the opening months of our relationship I'd put up with things which most people wouldn't have, such as Lissa going to hotels for cocaine blow-outs with another man and having private phone calls with her ex. If I backed out of publishing our story, how could I have any self-respect? I had to develop a spine at last. I had to go through with it for my own sake. That was enough to spur me on and I don't think I'd have been able to look myself in the eye ever again if I hadn't found the strength to publish.

The second volume was published on the 17th of January and two days later I left for Scotland. Having heard nothing after the release of the first, my agitation was rapidly fading. However, for a few weeks after my arrival, I still felt a touch of tension and nervousness each time my phone announced a message or call.

As time went by, I thought the agitation was gone for good. However, one evening in mid-March, I put a post on LinkedIn about *Volume 1: The Light Rises*. One of my contacts was a woman I'd contacted in order to try and uncover the truth of Lissa's activities at times it was likely she'd been lying. I'd messaged her by sending a connection request on that site and she'd informed Lissa of my contact, which had caused Lissa to ring on my first day at my mother's. This meant it was entirely possible she'd let Lissa know about the book when she saw my post.

That night I could barely sleep. The agitation had returned and was just as strong as ever. As soon as I woke the following morning, the post was deleted, but the agitation remained for a good few hours afterwards. It was this response at a point when I thought I'd healed enough not to have such feelings that caused me to finally seek professional help, but there'll be more on that later.

The symptom of agitation had its roots in our time together. I never knew where I stood with Lissa, never knew what mood she'd be in and what drama or issue may have befallen her. This lack of certainty and consistency had become elevated after she moved out of my Cornish cottage, when communication was restricted to our phones. Sometimes she'd claim bad reception had stopped her messaging, sometimes she'd blame her phone, at other times she'd promise a proper message or call later and then never keep those promises. Then there was the supposed struggle with her sexuality, which lasted from around mid-April 2021 right up until early July of that year and added a great deal to my feelings of uncertainty because, if she realised she was gay, our relationship would be over.

The agitation became even worse when she undertook her work placement on the Greek island and her treatment of me declined. By this point she'd started using the fact we were on the phone as a kind of weapon, hanging up if I irritated her.

Lissa's systematic abuse had left me entirely focussed on her. Because of this extrinsic focus and the intense confusion caused by her use of mixed messages and the attention-gaining strategy of playing the victim, I spent most of the spring, summer and early autumn of 2022 unable to do anything other than sit in my back yard. I was going over things again and again, in a state of turmoil as I tried to work out why her treatment of me was changing. One moment she was the Lissa I knew, the next she was replaced with a Lissa who had no regard for me. There was no solid ground and I was floundering, my mental state declining in equal measure to her treatment of me.

I feared confronting her about what was happening in case it made her even colder or caused her to walk away. I wondered what I could do to make things better, thinking that I had some control, some influence. In truth, I had none. It was all in her hands because she was holding all the strings, like a puppeteer controlling her marionette.

It's clear why I'd become so intensely focussed on Lissa and 'us.' It is also clear that this had been artificially created. It was the result of her abuse and deceits, and its strength was such that it lasted for a long time after our contact had come to an end.

Returning to Scotland, there was another sign of fear which soon became habitual. This was my regular habit of checking the driveway just in case she'd pulled up. I'd do so numerous times every day, whether I was inside or in the back garden. This is a common symptom of mental abuse known as 'hyper-vigilance.'

Unlike carrying the knife, this wasn't just out of fear, but also out of hope. I hoped she'd return to me and want to rekindle what we'd had. I had yet to accept that she'd never had any deep feelings for me, still held onto the heartfelt hope it had all been real.

It was thoroughly unrealistic, but there was so much I hadn't let go of at that time. I had loved her more profoundly than anyone else I'd ever been with and this made the act of release that much harder, especially when it came to the idea she'd felt the same about our relationship as I had. In reality, she'd likely not felt any particular connection, but had simply found it convenient. She was provided with a roof, support, company, affection, sex, and had made herself the centre of my focus. To Lissa, it was little more than the fulfilment of her wants until she decided what she wanted next.

Just like fear, love and hope are both potent forces, and all are often used by abusers to manipulate. Lissa had often encouraged thoughts of our future together when we were a couple, mentioning our marriage and having children. Throughout her time in my life, even in our last ever phone call, she also encouraged thoughts of adventures to come. Examples include a trip to Krakow and Prague which we'd been talking about for years, and a holiday at Disneyland Paris with her best-friend soulmate, Lissa claiming she'd always wanted to go with a 'significant other,' which implied my importance to her both then and in the future we envisaged.

All three emotions were entwined when it came to my constant vigilance, which included listening intently as every car passed on the road outside, waiting to see if they would slow and turn in. In fact, there was a point early in the process of writing this book when I had to get up and look out of the window after hearing a car with a similar engine pitch to hers slow down outside.

Realistically, she will not turn up out of the blue. Realistically, she won't want anything to do with me due to what the books reveal about her. The last thing on her 'to do' list would be to have contact with me, let alone to see me in person. Moreover, I shouldn't want to see her either.

My fear and paranoia was very apparent in relation to one of the deliveries I received in those early weeks. There'd been no notification and I wasn't expecting anything. Moreover, the drivers who'd previously dropped off packages had used the doorbell. The one who called late that particular evening decided to knock loudly instead, and just that simple change made all the difference.

Immediately feeling anxious, I got up and switched the outside lights on. Instead of simply opening the door as I usually did, I called 'who is it?' but there was no answer. All I could see was the light of a phone aimed at the front door from a few metres away.

I called out one or two more times. They still didn't answer, simply stood with their phone continuously aimed at the door. My heart was pounding, I was sweating and wide-eyed, stomach light and churning.

After what seemed like an age but was probably only around a minute or so, they finally left. Waiting for a while, I hesitantly opened the door to find a parcel placed on the step. It took quite a while to calm down after I'd taken it in and that occasion served to show how on edge I was in regards the potential of her or someone she knew coming to do me harm.

There were occasions when I'd go to the loo at night and imagine a brick crashing through the window, my presence discernible due to the light being turned on. I also sometimes imagined a brick or rock crashing through one of the lounge windows. I still feared attack, but my mind manifested it in a physical form.

I don't know how much fear would have played its part if I hadn't published our story. I think it would have been considerably less apparent and by far outweighed by love and hope. I would have been waiting for her to come back to me. In this light, it's probably healthier and more helpful to have felt so much fear. If I hadn't, I may have had more of a temptation to contact her. As you'll find in Chapter Seven, this is one of the temptations it's important to resist. For now, it's time to move on to the next layer of impact.

Chapter Four

Withdrawal

Withdrawal is a common symptom of mental abuse and the resulting trauma. This is hardly surprising as you've essentially been under attack and are undergoing mental and emotional extremes. You withdraw in order to regroup, to recover, to hide in order to avoid any further assaults. It's essentially like an animal retreating to lick its wounds, only wounds of this kind go largely unseen.

You also withdraw just to be able to cope with the internal chaos. Any other input from the outside world is too much to take on top of what's happening inside you. You need to be alone and cut yourself off. You need to disengage with the rest of society in order to simply get through the day without any additional stresses. The stress of what you're experiencing is hard enough to deal with on its own, any others would simply break the camel's back.

This leads to such things as not opening the post, not responding to emails or messages, not being able to cope with dealing with official correspondences, such as changes of address with the council, and not looking after yourself. In my case, I showered once every couple of weeks, and even that took an effort of will. I had to make myself, build myself up to it and find some reason why it had to be done, whether that was because I was expecting a delivery, going to have to visit the local store or going to have a therapy session. Opening the post was also tackled in fits and starts and my inability to face it had begun back in the spring of 2022, when Lissa's treatment of me had started to decline. I hadn't been able to spare the mental energy on letters from the bank, council, government or anyone else. It had all been used to try and fathom what was happening and in trying to create messages and Snaps which would lift her mood and bring back the Lissa I knew. The extrinsic focus she'd been creating right from the start had me in its vicelike grip and had tightened its hold from May 2022 onwards. This continued in Scotland.

I withdrew from interacting with pretty much the rest of humanity other than my close friends and mother. Sometimes, even contacting them or responding to messages they'd sent to me was hard. I was trying to deal with so much internally that I struggled to be able to write a normal message to anyone. It was as if words had no meaning unless they related to what I was going through. Anything else wasn't important or took too much energy, which was being totally sapped by the impact of the abuse and what I'd discovered about Lissa's clandestine behaviour when we were a couple. Conjuring the ability to communicate about anything else was virtually impossible back then.

Of course, it was important to keep these channels of communication open. In many instances, the people messaging were really just trying to make sure I was okay without continually asking that question. I couldn't see this in the early months. I couldn't see anything. I was in darkness and didn't realise the messages of friends and family were actually beams of light filled with concern and love.

My self-esteem had been purposefully targeted by Lissa and this was also part of the reason for my withdrawal. I'd become so negative about my appearance that I wanted to hide my face from everyone. While still at my mother's, I'd kept my head bowed and eyes averted when visiting the nearby supermarket. When I had met other people's gazes, I was guarded and expected to find derision, disgust or even horror in their eyes, such was the state of my confidence.

In Scotland, I was afforded the opportunity to avoid human contact other than over the phone or briefly at the door when the postman or delivery drivers called. I still considered how they must be seeing me, thinking they probably saw me as a strange man and, though I was sometimes grateful for a little human interaction, on the whole, simply wanted to be left alone.

On the few walks I went on, when a car passed by I'd imagine what they were thinking of the odd man walking alongside the road. Thankfully, I saw no one in person, but found myself alone on the coast, left to my thoughts of Lissa and what she'd done.

There was an intrusion upon my withdrawal in the second week of being in Scotland. A friend who lived in Gretna Green came to visit with his partner one afternoon. I didn't feel ready for company, but hadn't wanted to appear rude in declining his offer to drive the considerable distance in order to see me.

When they arrived, I settled into his presence with ease, having been friends for over twenty years. However, I was wary of his partner, who'd I'd not met before. I was conscious of how she'd regard me, but tried to relax, just to be myself. However, 'myself' at that time wasn't the person he'd previously known, but a man barely holding on.

Whenever I began to speak about Lissa, my friend would shut me down, stating that it was time to move on, to get on with my life. This was one of a number of occasions when I found people saying such things and I became aware that they didn't realise the importance of speaking it out in such circumstances. They weren't trying to be hurtful or uncaring in any way, they just didn't know how intense, confusing and tumultuous mental abuse can be, and that the victim needs to be able to talk about it, partly so as to release the pressure and partly because it's a way of trying to figure things out.

This said, another aspect of withdrawal which reared its head, was my withdrawal from talking about these things with friends and family. Though I couldn't help but talk about Lissa to some degree, I tried to curtail how much I said as I was worried that people were probably becoming irritated by it.

This began to shut down an important avenue of expressing the confusion and chaos. Thankfully, as this began to become more apparent, the phone calls to my mother dwindling and my messages to friends likewise falling away, therapy stepped in, but more of that later.

If you're a victim of abuse, try and keep these lines of communication open. I'm not underestimating the situation when I say they can genuinely be life lines. There were times when, if I hadn't been able to pick up the phone and talk to someone, I would have been overcome with despair and may not have made it to this point. One thing to bear in mind is that the calls and messages you receive are signs of love. People love you. People care about you. Don't you ever forget that.

If you're a friend or family member of someone who's been mentally abused, then keep going. Don't give up because you think they're not letting go and moving on. Don't give up because you think observations about their abuser are falling on deaf ears, either before the abuse has come to an end or after. My mother and at least a couple of friends were telling me that Lissa was abusing me, manipulating me and was a terrible person long before our contact came to an end. Though there was no sign that their words were having any effect, I think they were slowly helping me see the truth. It took time because of the love I felt for her and the highly effective persona of being a vulnerable, anxious victim with a kind heart which she presents to the world. I had to come to a place when I could see beyond the woman I loved to the real woman hidden beneath that mask.

I would also say that if the person you know who's been abused starts to talk about it less or stops altogether, be aware this may not be a sign they're healing and moving on. It may be they're worried they've talked about it too much, that they're aware they keep repeating themselves as they try to wrestle with the reality which has come crashing through the illusion of who the other person pretends to be. Make sure they know they can continue talking about it, that you don't mind if they repeat themselves. Your presence in their life may just be the thing which saves it, as was the case with Sandi in relation to me.

She is a retiree who takes her dog, Sky, for walks every morning and we'd met while I was out with my camera early in the spring of 2022, while things were still okay with Lissa. We'd become friends and would meet up for walks around three times a week, sometimes more.

As Lissa's treatment of me began to decline, she became the focus of every walk. I was unable to hold in my feelings of confusion, hurt, dismay and general heartache as I tried to puzzle out what was happening. Sandi would offer advice, make comments about Lissa's behaviour and be prepared to spend the entire duration of each walk consumed by talk of the events taking place.

Because these walks were early in the day, I was able to vent some of the pressure and this allowed me to endure the hours of extrinsic focus ahead of me. If I hadn't had this vent, I don't think I'd be here now, such was the intensity of those times and the continual mistreatment conducted by Lissa.

So, don't give up on the person who's going through so much turmoil. Try and understand just how consuming it must be and allow them to talk about it. Let them know you're there. Let them know they're not alone.

When it comes to Scotland, my withdrawal drew me further into myself and into the cocoon of the house. I retreated from the world but, thanks to the fear and paranoia discussed in the previous chapter, was on constant alert. The knife carrying and general vigilance were like the physical expression of how I felt mentally. I needed to defend what was left. This defence, along with the need to come to terms with the confusion and the clash of what I'd thought we'd shared with the truth of what she'd been doing, were enough to make me reclusive. The world beyond the house was too much to handle on top of everything else.

This withdrawal was mainly the result of the impact of all that had been discovered, though healing was taking place in small ways. As the force of that impact lessened, the healing increased and the balance began to shift. However, the wish to hide away remained for around three months and there's still a residue of it now.

Looking back, I'm aware how badly I regarded myself. Whenever I looked in the mirror I'd see myself negatively and even sometimes vocalised negative comments, such as 'ugly bastard.' Because Lissa had targeted my already low self-esteem, I was unable to see myself in a good light when it comes to my appearance. Sadly, I'm aware that making those statements helped perpetuate my self-disgust and recall that I'd often pull a face at myself just to prove how ugly I was.

Statements can be powerful. They serve to reinforce the thoughts behind them. This means those thoughts are more likely to persist and affect how you both view yourself and behave. But, if statements can undermine, they can also strengthen.

Many people use positive statements, often calling them 'affirmations.' Some have mantras they say to themselves at the start of the day or before important meetings. Gestures can also be used to reinforce them, just as my gesture of pulling a face was used to reinforce the negative statements. For example, you could simply look in the mirror and state, 'I *will* get through this,' and as you say the words nod to yourself. This genuinely gives the words more power because the affirmation isn't just words, its words and actions. The emphasis on 'will' actually helps too because you're reinforcing it with conviction.

Give it a try. It can genuinely help and start to change the way you perceive yourself. Don't let what they made you think about yourself win out. That would be a victory for your abuser. Instead, use this simple method to help undo what they've done to you. Maybe have a look at some positive affirmations online, just don't forget to give yourself a nod when saying them to yourself. Approve of yourself.

Have you got your nodding head on? Right, get ready to nod and emphasise. Repeat after me; 'I *am* worthwhile and I *will* make it through.'

Chapter Five

Stuckness

What is stuckness? It's linked to the lack of motivation I mentioned in the previous chapter, the one that caused me to be an unwashed Ed with a mountain of post which would make Everest jealous. It's as if the air is as thick as soup, making everything feel like it takes great effort. It's a sense of being stuck in a state of emotional pain and hopelessness from which there seems no escape, but there is.

Every time I got up from the settee, DVDs of television series endlessly playing in the background, I felt heavy and ponderous. It was as if someone had turned up the gravity. Every movement felt like it took all my energy.

At the same time, it felt like I was going nowhere mentally and emotionally. Nothing seemed different. Nothing seemed to change. I was still wrestling with the same things that had been constantly going around my head and clenching my heart during the stay at my mother's.

I was physically and psychologically stuck. I didn't want to be. I wanted the weight to lift and desperately wanted the thoughts and feelings to ease. It was so consuming that there were numerous occasions when I simply didn't want to be here anymore. I was barely coping with the intensity and continuous nature of what was happening within. I just wanted some release, even if only a temporary respite in order to gather my strength, but with wintry conditions outside and no friends who could accompany me in any way other than over the phone, my stuckness was accentuated.

This isn't to say I didn't value calls or messages, only that they are no substitute for someone's company, and this was the first prolonged period without company or at least regular daily contact for over four and a half years. Lissa had not only left a gaping hole into which I fell, she'd already created the darkness within it, one which meant I couldn't see a way out.

You know there was, otherwise you wouldn't be reading this book. This means that if you're experiencing similar feelings, you can be certain the stuckness will lift. The weight lessens until you end up looking back and seeing how strong you were to be able to cope with such distress on every level. That's because you *are* amazing (nod, emphasise and say 'Yes, I *am* amazing').

It took time, as all these processes do. I barely noticed it was receding, though I did notice little signs of change, some of which will be mentioned in Chapter Eight: *Stepping Stones*. They were signs of recovery, but stuckness is primarily related to the impact.

It was a dark and lonely place to be mentally and emotionally, one accentuated by my hyper-vigilance and withdrawal. All these symptoms compound each other, making the situation all but impossible. It is no wonder that the aspects of everyday life, like responding to messages and opening the post, were shut down to a large degree. In order to function even on the most basic level, other avenues which demanded mental energy had to be closed while the main street of my existence was being reconstructed after being demolished by what I'd discovered, the abuse of the previous four years and the increase in its intensity during the last four months or so of our contact.

I can imagine my life as a small town which contains buildings, statues and features representing the various elements and their importance to me. For over four years a statue of Lissa had graced the middle of the town square. Once, when we'd lived together, I'd stood beside her, our hands clasped. My Cornish cottage stood nearby, garden filled with wildlife and interior with fond memories, the rolling countryside and coastline visible beyond. A library was off the square, its shelves filled with the books I'd written and a table illuminated by a shaft of inspiration's light at its centre where my laptop rested in readiness for new works to be created. An open-air exhibition of my photography was located in an orchard off the main square, my pictures hanging from tree branches and propped up amidst the undergrowth, each capturing a moment of beauty in nature. There was a café where my friends were seated; light, airy and filled with smiles. Some of their houses, those that were close enough to visit, were down the side streets. The two village pubs were there too. My mother's and father's houses were present and my cats, Natiri and Zennor, sat in the sunshine beneath the statue. The streets themselves consisted of grass filled with wildflowers and lined with trees. Birdsong filled the air and insects hummed the tune of pollination, the air filled with the scent of flowers and blossom.

That place was no more. It was a blackened ruin beneath dark skies choked with cloud and the dust of destruction. Pieces of the walls continued to crumble and nature was silent as I sat in the middle of the square with the remains of the statue. I wanted to piece it back together more than anything else. My heart yearned for it, but my mind was in confusion, finding two versions of Lissa's face in the rubble. One was smiling and the other's expression was filled with disdain. I couldn't decide which belonged on the statue, believed for a time that it was both, it's just that one had been hidden, turned away from me at all times. I also couldn't fathom how the person the statue symbolised had brought about the ruination of everything around me, was in shock and dumbfounded by the extent of what she'd done.

That's where I was then, still coming to terms with everything, still trying to work out why and how the centre of my existence had transformed into the destroyer of it. My stuckness was anchored to that confusion. I was holding the two faces and looking about at the rubble, unable to work out who Lissa was or how to put everything back together.

As this internal struggle continued, there was little room to consider anything external. I was immobilised by the immensity of the task, didn't know where to start. At least, that's what I thought. Now, I can see that just the act of trying to work things out was part of the process. I needed to go through it and, I promise you, it does pass and you start to rebuild the town of your life.

I'm writing this in early May, around two months since the stuckness stated to noticeably lift. I now know the face which belongs on the statue is the one of disdain and the pieces of that statue have been removed to the outskirts of town, slowly being covered over by vegetation. The smiling face has been placed in a garden of remembrance down a side street. The plants there have yet to grow, have yet to call me to visit, but I hope one day that the fact it was real for me will be enough.

The café is active again and the door to my parents' houses wide open. The wildlife and greenery has returned to the streets, though there is still more growth to come. The library is in use, as these words bear testament to. What's more, there's a new statue in the middle of the square. Do you know who it is? It's me! What's more,

I'm larger than before, symbolising growing strength and self-confidence. Maybe one day another figure will stand beside me, but until then, I stand there with the cats at my sides and wild birds perched upon my shoulders. Oh yes, and there's a butterfly fluttering about my head, along with a huge bear with his arms crossed standing behind me. The look on his face is one which lets everyone know, 'this is Ed and you *will* respect who he is.'

What would the town of your heart and head look like? What happened to it due to the abuse? What has caused your stuckness? Maybe you can draw a plan of your town as it was, as it is or, most importantly, how you see it in the future. See what buildings are still standing. See what you value in your life. Erect a statue of yourself in the square, that's the place to start, and then set to the rebuilding process. It can and does happen. Your town can be filled with life once more.

Chapter Six

Loops

Loops are closely related to stuckness and operate on the mental, emotional and physical levels. In relation to the latter, there were a number of behavioural loops in which I was caught in those early weeks in Scotland. All had their roots in the final months of contact with Lissa. There were three in particular. The first related to food, the second to my viewing choices and the third to sleeping arrangements.

During the summer of 2022, I began to eat the same food every night at least four times a week. This was a particular brand and type of frozen pizza. I even asked my local store to get more in stock so as to maintain this level of consumption. They were quick to cook and eat, requiring the minimal amount mental energy to be expended.

The temporary move to my mother's saw a change in diet, but the creation of a new loop. Instead of the particular frozen pizza, she would make me either fried or scrambled eggs on toast virtually every night. This lasted for the entire three months I stayed with her despite there being a drawer full of other options especially for me in her freezer.

At that time, I wasn't able to maintain a vegan diet, my mind unable to cope with buying and cooking food, so went back to being vegetarian for the time being. I couldn't even handle making choices as to what to eat, so went with what was easy and quick for my mother to make. When she'd mention the fact I was eating the same thing, thinking that surely I wanted something else for a change, I'd adamantly refuse. Trying to explain, I said that I couldn't even bear the thought of having anything different, stating that it was comfort food. However, it was much more than that.

It was a sign that my mental energy was totally consumed by what was happening. It was also a retreat into routine, something which allowed me to function.

This food loop continued once I arrived in Scotland, though became a little more varied. I returned to buying the same pizza I'd been eating in Cornwall though, due to relying on home deliveries, couldn't buy enough to be eaten every night. I started eating a simple meal I'd not had for many years and had been common when I was a child. Porridge oats with drinking chocolate mixed in and then oat milk added (think choclatey porridge), this really was comfort food.

As the days and weeks passed, the variety of food increased. This reflected a decrease in the amount of angst I was feeling, along with a decrease in confusion in regards Lissa and what she'd done. My thoughts were still predominantly about her and our time together, but other thoughts were starting to take root. I considered what I wanted to do to the garden in order to make it a space rich in habitat and biodiversity. I thought about moving forward with renewable energy installation. I wondered what to do with the static caravan in the back garden. I thought about this book and others to come after, along with whether I wanted to continue writing. Each thought which didn't relate to Lissa, our past or the things she'd done was like a seedling bursting through the frozen soil of thoughts in which I'd been stuck for so long. They were signs of a gentle thaw.

The second loop related to what DVDs I was watching. When Lissa was on the Greek island there was only a small selection I could view while her treatment of me steadily declined, which included Disney's *Moana* and *The Lone Ranger*, both of which she'd introduced me to. Once she returned to the U.K. and the revival of our closeness which I'd hoped for never materialised, I took to watching recent James Bond films on repeat as she treated me with growing unkindness and open cruelty, sometimes with an undertone of amusement.

On rainy days, in the evenings and all through the night, they would play over and over again. It was a way to distract my mind, especially when I tried to sleep. Instead of thinking about what had and was happening, I could focus on the familiar dialogue and sounds of action in order to find sleep.

This changed when I got to my mother's. Writing the story of our time together completely drained me. I was consumed by thoughts of her and us as I wrote about the wonderful times and the terrible ones. Our daily four year contact had ended in September and seen a brief re-emergence in the middle of October, shortly after which I began writing. I suppose, in a way, it was like keeping the contact going. Every single day I'd be up between four and six in the morning and start work after a coffee or two, not stopping until six in the evening apart from in times of distress, of which there were many.

When the evenings came, I found I couldn't watch movies. Even the thought filled me with a mild sense of dread. Watching them had been the most common shared experience Lissa and I had enjoyed. It had been precious and filled with comments, theories as to plot twists, Internet Movie Database checks, smiles, laughter, tears and lots of physical closeness, the two of us commonly snuggling together. I simply couldn't entertain the thought of putting on any movies without her there.

Instead, my mother would record episodes of four different detective series during the days and we'd then watch one or two each evening. I'd do so from a different settee as I rolled cigarettes ready for the following day's work. This lasted the entire time I was there and I felt quite guilty and a little sad that I'd been unable to watch any movies with her as it was something we'd enjoyed doing every time she'd visited me in Cornwall.

When I got to Scotland, the same loop continued. I'd purchased two of the series my mother and I had been watching, getting boxed sets of every season. They were playing all day and all night. Unable to do much else due to being consumed by thoughts of Lissa and us, I had them on both for company and the limited distraction they provided, and this ended up lasting the first couple of months.

Then came a change and the TV was often turned off during the days and while I was sleeping. This was evidence that my mind was starting to settle, though my emotions weren't.

The loop relating to sleep began at the start of the week of my 50th birthday in late August 2022 and was connected with needing to play DVDs all night. Because of the trauma caused by Lissa's worsening treatment, I found myself unable to settle in bed. My mind wouldn't allow it.

From then on, I ended up sleeping on the three-seater settee in the lounge with films playing on loops through the nights. This continued even at my mother's, though without the company of DVDs.

Though I managed to sleep in bed for the first few nights of my stay, I soon found myself bedding down on one of the couches. This then remained the case for the rest of the time I was there. Even though it was winter and I'd sometimes wake up very cold, I didn't return to the bed, but persisted with sleeping clothed and in my dressing gown, both my cats joining me, as they had on my settee in Cornwall.

There was no change once I arrived in Scotland, something aided and abetted by the fact I didn't buy a mattress until I'd been there for around a month. Even after it arrived, I still remained on the same three-seater which had been my place of rest in Cornwall, the DVDs playing all through the night.

I tried to sleep in bed on a couple of occasions during the first two months, both times without success. I was restless and my mind wouldn't let me sleep, soon finding myself returning to the distraction offered in the lounge. However, at least there was a willingness to try.

It wasn't until 8th April that I finally managed to spend a night sleeping in bed. The TV and lights still on in the lounge, the door was left open and I found myself drifting off. When I woke in the morning it was with a smile. I'd done it at last and that was one of many small milestones that signified recovery was taking place. Though it didn't signal a return to sleeping in bed every night, it did show things were changing and, from that point on, where I slept depended on how I was feeling rather than automatically returning to the couch.

I think this loop, along with being connected to the need for distraction, was also related to the fact Lissa and I had shared a bed for two and a half years. The fact I still needed to sleep on a couch at my mother's even without DVD assistance points to this being the case. She was the first partner I've had with whom I cuddled up every night as we drifted off. Our physical closeness was far greater than anything I'd experienced before and was one of the precious elements of the relationship. It even remained once we became best-friend soulmates, the two of us continuing to sleep naked and cuddle up together. I missed her presence next to me when watching films and at night when going to bed in Cornwall prior to starting to sleep on the couch. I'd look to where she'd once rested beside me and wish I could see the covers moving as she breathed or feel the gentle twitch of a leg as she dreamt. Though the distraction of DVDs was the main reason for abandoning my bed, I'm sure this also played a part.

This and the food loops make me think of Einstein. He had numerous sets of exactly the same clothes, saying he didn't want to waste mental effort on picking what to wear each day. In my case, I think those loops were partly due to not having the mental energy to spare. It was all being used by my extrinsic focus, along with all the emotions I was going through. There was no energy to even consider different foods and there was also none by which to think about brushing my teeth, washing my face, making my way to the bedroom and getting undressed. It was easier both mentally and physically simply to stay in my clothes and on the settee. It was the path of least resistance, and that's the path I followed in regards everything as I tried to deal with my internal crisis. This is echoed in not opening my post, the withdrawal and the lack of motivation which was part of stuckness.

These behavioural loops and others, such as checking the driveway, all slowly came undone. They reflected my mental and emotional states, which could be described as a cyclone. The high winds and debris had been constantly circling since the summer of 2022, all but blocking out other sights and sounds. As those winds slowly calmed and sometimes even dropped away, the loops started to break and I could hear the words of friends and family, along with those of my therapist. I could hear the birdsong and appreciate the peacefulness of my location. I was starting to let the world back in. At the same time, the debris was beginning to clear, bringing me greater clarity, not only in regards Lissa and us, but my situation and the potential it held for a contented life in harmony with the rest of the natural world.

These loops afforded security and routine when they were needed. The food loop helped reduce the demands of normal day-to-day existence while my mind was otherwise occupied. The choice of viewing helped me avoid any unnecessary increase in trauma that may have arisen from watching films, which could have triggered memories or caused me to think of Lissa. They also provided some distraction so that I could, even if only for a moment, find brief release from thoughts about her. This viewing loop coupled with the sleeping loop allowed me to find rest at a time when it was hard to quiet my mind. All three helped me through the worst of her treatment of me while she was still in my life and also helped me through the worst of the turmoil after our contact had ended. They were safety precautions taken out of necessity, helping to reduce the extreme mental and emotional pressure of those times.

I didn't have to consciously break the food loop, it simply came undone at its own pace, one in line with my recovery. The DVD loop was broken by watching a particular film one day, which I'm going to speak about in *Stepping Stones*. The sleep loop is still being broken, and has been the only one to require conscious effort. It's easy just to return to the settee every night after having my final coffee. The habit has been made and, even without the TV on most nights, it's an effort to break. This is partly because there have been other periods in my life when I've slept on the settee and I genuinely find it very comfortable. Even so, this loop is fading too.

Getting stuck in loops of behaviour isn't necessarily a bad thing. In my case, they were helping to lessen the strength of the cyclone by providing distraction, which in essence was helping to preserve my sanity. They were also helping me find rest, which is vitally important, along with continuing to eat.

My loops were harmless and necessary to get me through. There are probably damaging and destructive loops too. If you find yourself looping in any way, be sure to talk to someone if it's something which concerns you or is having an adverse effect. A helpful loop is one thing, but an unhelpful one could turn into a downward spiral and that's going to prolong and potentially worsen the situation.

There is one very negative loop that I experienced other than those related to my paranoia. Like those, it was a mental loop. I would simply imagine shooting myself in the head with a pistol, holding my hand to my head as if it were a gun. This was commonly when I rested my head on the cushion of the settee in order to try and find sleep.

Initially, this loop went undetected; I didn't even notice I was doing it. Once I did, I knew it had to stop. Not only was it encouraging thoughts of taking my own life, but it was also encouraging thoughts of me not being worthwhile. Thankfully, once I became aware of it, I soon put an end to it.

Another unhealthy mental loop was caused by Lissa's undermining of my already low self-esteem when it comes to my looks. Whenever I looked in the mirror, I'd be unkind about myself, as mentioned. Though I realised what I was doing, it took longer than the 'gun loop' for me to take action because I was so down on myself. When I did, I started to chastise myself whenever I was nasty about my looks and, in time, began to see myself in a more positive light. This would have taken longer if I hadn't broken the negative reinforcement of this loop.

So, if you get caught in loops, check they're not reinforcing any negative thoughts or feelings and make sure they're not damaging in any other way. Search out the reasons for the loops and check they don't tick any of these boxes. If they don't, they're likely to have been created as a means to get you through, to ease the burden of trying to live an everyday life while coping with the trauma of abuse. They do come undone given time, but do seek assistance if you have any concerns.

Chapter Seven

Resisting Temptation

The title of this chapter may suggest something Biblical and it's actually the case that its content definitely has implications in regards the wellbeing of your soul. This is because there are a number of temptations which I believe are vitally important to resist while you're recovering from mental abuse. These are; 1. Contacting your abuser. 2. Checking your abuser's social media. 3. Getting drunk. 4. Seeking someone new.

1. At no point did I contact Lissa after our goodbyes had been said. This was in spite of keeping her number on my phone and not blocking her. This meant that at any time I could have tried calling, texting or messaging via Whatsapp. I could have also emailed her or, if desperate, reactivated my Facebook or started an Instagram page in order to try and make contact. I did none of the above.

One of the reasons was the fear that's already been discussed. Another was that if I discovered she'd blocked my number it would add to my devastation. Yet another was because I knew I'd be placing myself in a position of weakness if I broke the silence and she would be aware that she was still in control. Then there was the continuing agitation I felt at the thought of communicating with her.

Contacting her would not have been good for my mental health at the time. It would have set me back and only helped to stir things up. It would have brought so much back to the surface of my mind and meant the healing process took that much longer.

To be honest, the occasions when I did think of contacting her were few and far between because of the anxiety I felt just at the thought of doing so. Yes, I would have dearly loved to hear her voice, but not in a frustrated, angry, distressed or indignant way. I wanted to hear the smile in her words or to hear her singing to me, as she once had on a regular basis, neither of which was realistic considering what had happened. Both were sorely missed, as was the sound of her laughter, but they'd actually been largely vacant for a good few months before our contact ended. They weren't going to magically return. There was nothing to be gained from breaking the silence, only ground to be lost as it would be a backward step.

The same is true in any case of mental abuse. By breaking the silence, you immediately place your abuser in a position of power and yourself in a position of weakness. Despite what they've done, you've initiated contact. You've tried to break away from them and yet returned. This puts them in the driver's seat once again, but with more confidence than before. They are also potentially able to cause you great pain, seeing your vulnerability and exploiting it, possibly being cruel and even rejecting you.

The silence may be painful, but what they could do if you try to contact them would hurt far more. If you get tempted to contact them, contact a friend, family member or even one of the organisations listed in Appendix III instead. Think about what your abuser has done. Think about your internal town and the destruction they've caused. Say to yourself, 'I will *not* contact them,' and shake your head. Find something which works for you and resist the urge.

2. There was never any temptation to look at Lissa's social media. Quite simply, I couldn't take the pain of seeing her simply getting on with her life as if I didn't matter in the slightest, which is exactly what I expected to find. I already suspected she had never loved me and probably used me from the outset, and didn't need further proof of how little she felt for me.

The only time I saw something in relation to her was when she changed her Whatsapp profile picture, and that was painful enough as it was. To see posts and photographs on social media would have been unbearable.

The picture was simple; she was looking back with a smile as she walked along the waterfront in Belfast. It felt like she was saying, 'look at me, I'm happy to be leaving you behind.' That thought didn't bring the most pain. That was caused by the wish it had been me with her, me taking the photograph, me who she was smiling at. The idea that it was her new partner, whose existence she'd tried to hide from me in the final weeks of our friendship, was also something which stabbed at me.

That experience was enough to confirm that looking at her social media would be tortuous and only give rise to further pain. I also didn't want to hear about what she was doing from anyone else and told a couple of my friends to please not tell me if they ever found out. Thankfully, they had no more wish to look at her profiles than I did, all bar none wanting nothing to do with her.

Again, use things that work for you in order to resist checking your abuser's social media profiles. The majority of people put their best faces on and display the best sides of their lives when it comes to their profiles. This means all you're likely to see are smiles and good things in your abuser's life. This is going to sting even though it's what you'd find on most profiles.

If you need to block them in order not to look, then that's what you should do. If you can't bring yourself to do so, then get a friend to do it for you if the temptation feels like it may get too strong. Let your friends and family know you don't want to know if they see or hear anything about your abuser.

Friends and family, don't pass on anything about what the abuser is doing. Allow the victim their space and time to heal. Updating them on what the person who's caused so much pain and turmoil is doing does not help at all, even if they're going through tough times themselves. It may seem like a good thing to share if they are, but it will simply bring the abuser to mind in a present tense. Instead, let them fall away into the past. Let the healing take place and the victim move on.

In relation to social media in general, it can be a bit of a double-edged sword. During the final months of contact, posting my nature photography on Twitter helped serve as a distraction from the torment. When Lissa initially cut ties, I found I couldn't post anymore, even the thought of doing so making me feel anxious. This is probably because it had been one of the threads woven into those dark times.

I started posting again sometime later, sporadically at first, but my posts becoming more regular. By the beginning of May 2023, I was often contributing as my general confidence grew. However, this was somewhat undermined on the 3rd of that month. I'd surprised myself and taken my first selfie for over seven months. Feeling happy with it, I updated my profile picture and didn't receive a single like, which wasn't good for someone piecing together their self-esteem.

So, take note of your reactions to interactions on social media. Avoid anything which has a negative effect and seek out the positive. It's a fragile time and it's best to only engage with things which will help you heal and grow stronger.

3. Temptation number three involves alcohol. By extension, it also includes any other drugs. I described it as 'getting drunk' above, but the key word in regards this temptation is; 'excess.' Don't drink or use drugs excessively. They are not a crutch. They will not help you limp along. Instead, taken to excess, they will trip you over and you may end up flat on your face for quite some time.

I did not drink anything in the three months I was at my mother's other than a sip of sloe gin and a couple of tots of Baileys Irish Cream at my sister's on Christmas Day. That was literally all I had, even though I was given a number of bottles of alcohol as gifts.

Once I got to Scotland, the story didn't change. This was despite having a substantial collection when adding what I brought from my mother's to what had been in storage, including three bottles of my favourite drink; spiced rum. My bottle rack was full and the overflow was placed in the cabinet beneath. I even purchased more while I was still entertaining the idea that one day Lissa would visit or come to live here, imagining us getting tipsy while listening to music, as we'd regularly done in Cornwall. At no point were any of the bottles opened.

Though they remained sealed, I did have the occasional drink. I bought small pre-mixed cans of Malibu and cola despite owning large bottles of both. This was because the pre-mixed drinks were comparatively weak. I also knew that opening a bottle could lead to the temptation to finish it and so purposefully limited myself to the cans, having two at most on any given evening and only drinking rarely.

Alcohol is a depressant. Lots of alcohol is also likely to make you more emotional and less inhibited. This means you're more likely to contact your abuser if the temptation arises while drunk or to look at their social media, thereby causing you to submit to two further temptations. If you're really unlucky, it could cause you to sleep with someone, which would be succumbing to all four at once.

The sad fact is that many movies and series show people turning to drink when the brown stuff hits the fan. This common portrayal normalises such behaviour and many people reach for the bottle in such circumstances. It's not the right thing to do. It will not help. You will end up taking longer to recover and it won't just be the trauma you'll need to recover from, but the hangovers, paranoia and other side effects of drug use.

Trust me, alcohol doesn't numb how you feel. In truth, it can have the opposite effect and accentuate your emotions. That's not a good thing to do when they're already in such turmoil. So, leave the bottles on the supermarket shelves or unopened if they're already on yours. If you think you might turn to them, if they start to tempt you, give them over to someone else's care or even pour them down the sink.

If you do end up drunk once or twice, don't chastise yourself. Understand yourself and remove any further temptation. If you see people turning to drink in a film or series, just shake your head and see the state it gets them into. Yes, there are those that say drink or other drugs can numb the pain, but that's simply not the case in my experience. It has the opposite effect and makes you more susceptible to breaking down whilst also making you physically unwell. So, ignore the stereotype and avoid the drink, you'll feel better for it in the long-run.

4. When it comes to seeing someone new, I'd strongly advise against it during the impact stage of mental abuse and at least the early stages of the healing process. This is because it holds the potential to not only damage yourself, but also someone else. It's important to be well along the road to recovery before you seek out new potential relationships and to know yourself enough to realise when you're genuinely ready.

Of the four temptations, this is the one I found hardest to resist despite being adamant that I'd never engage in a relationship again. By their very nature, they all come to an end one way or another and I didn't think I could take the heartache of another loss.

The vacuum left by Lissa was enormous and there were times I'd have done anything to have her back in my life in any capacity, let alone as a partner. I struggled to cope with the silence of my phone after over four years of regular daily contact. She was the love of my life and had been the centre of my existence for so long. In her place was suddenly emptiness. I teetered on its brink, trying not to fall into the utter darkness waiting there.

To try and stop myself, I joined one of the most popular dating sites in the U.K. while at my mother's. I told myself that I'd simply signed up in order to meet people who lived in the area of Scotland I'd be moving to. I indicated that I was looking for 'friendship' but, deep down, knew I wanted someone to make me feel loved again, someone to snuggle up with, to walk with in nature, to make me feel happy and complete again, someone to experience life with and take away my feeling of isolation as Lissa once had.

There were a number of reasons why this wasn't the right thing to do. The first is that no one could have filled Lissa's shoes at the time, partly because she knew me better than anyone else and I her. Any new relationship by its very nature starts the opposite way around; with you barely knowing each other. Lissa and I also shared a vast amount of common ground, far more than any other relationship I'd ever had, so it was unlikely I'd find it with another. Further, who I really wanted was Lissa and so anyone else would have merely been a substitute rather than a partner in their own right.

It also wasn't the right course of action because I wasn't in a fit state mentally or emotionally to be engaging in another relationship. I had yet to deal with the trauma or to move on. I was still clinging onto hopes of Lissa returning in spite of what she'd put me through. The battle between the persona she portrays and the woman I'd discovered behind it was still taking place, the two Lissa's locked in a struggle that had me caught in the no man's land between.

This just goes to show that it would have been unfair of me to lead anyone into believing I was looking for a relationship. In fact, it's likely that doing so would have ended up making me feel worse about myself. I had to be honest; I was nowhere near ready. When I accepted that, I cancelled my membership and came off the site. Thankfully, I hadn't pursued or flirted with anyone in particular, telling myself I'd leave it up to fate, so no damage had been done to others. This was an important step to take for my own wellbeing and that of a potential new partner.

If you manage to resist one of these temptations, that's great. Resisting two is even better. Three is brilliant. Four is simply awesome. At the same time, don't feel bad if you succumb. It's understandable. Recovery from mental abuse is a hard thing to do, especially if you still feel a strong bond with your abuser. Just try and be kind on yourself and know you'll get stronger.

Chapter Eight

Stepping Stones

Now that you've read the 'impact chapters,' it's time for the 'recovery chapters' to begin. The recovery process consists of lots of stepping stones; events which act as markers of your progress as you slowly mend and find your way back from the damage and cruelty.

Sometimes there may be a large gap between one stepping stone and the next, but that's okay. It may be it's a particularly momentous stone to reach and other things are necessary before the step can be taken, such as acceptance or increased strength. On occasion, you may linger on a particular stone, and that's okay too. You may need a little time to let the realisation or change settle and become more solid. Whether there's a gap or pause, they're necessary within the general current of forward motion. You may feel that it's passing you by, but that's not the case. It's a current that slows and speeds up, but it's also a current that can't be escaped; the current of time. Yes, it's a cliché, but it really is a great healer. As the distance grows between then and now, the impact of the abuse concurrently lessens.

It wasn't only darkness I had to escape from in the early months of recovery. At that time, I also saw a great deal of brightness relating to our time together. I thought Lissa and I had shared far more good times than bad, and the idea that I'd never experience new ones with her was extremely hard to accept. The time we lived together at the cottage and the times in each other's company after she'd moved out were seen as the best of my life.

This meant recovery was twofold; both from the trauma of her words and actions, and the trauma of losing something I'd thought more precious than anything else I'd ever experienced. I had to come to terms with the former and see the latter for what it truly was; time spent with someone who was taking advantage of, cheating on, lying to and abusing me, no matter the smiles and laughter masking this truth.

It makes it more complicated when you still love the one who abused you. This is partly because you try to understand why they treated you in such a way. I'd given her my time and love, the two most precious things I could give. I'm gentle, kind and compassionate, and yet she'd treated me appallingly. Coping with this was hard, but the stepping stones I reached showed me that recovery was starting to take place, even though it often felt like nothing was changing.

Some days I didn't feel like I could take much more. When I was writing the books, I made some horrendous discoveries in regards what she'd done and felt that if I found out one more thing I would fall apart. I was close to snapping, to completely breaking down, but that line was not crossed.

And here I am now, writing this book. That in itself shows that things move on, that healing happens, and it happens with each passing day. Even if you don't feel any different, you are. Look for the small stepping stones which point to this fact. You won't see them coming, especially in the darker, earlier stages of impact and recovery, so you need to stay alert to them. Some are small and can pass without notice unless you're looking out for signs of change. When you do notice, you know that a new threshold has been reached, that you are moving on and, even though you can't see the path ahead, there are more stepping stones waiting to take you farther along the road to rediscovering yourself.

I remember a very simple stepping stone which occurred early in April. I looked in the mirror and smiled at myself. It was that simple. Yet it was a step, a sign of change.

Usually, I looked at myself in misery, disgust or dislike, something encouraged by Lissa's mistreatment. To smile at myself and feel good about how I looked was an unexpected change, one that I only realised as I walked out of the bathroom. The realisation itself caused me to laugh and broadened my grin. It felt so good to see myself positively for a change.

So you see, these stepping stones can easily pass by unnoticed. If you remain alert to them, your confidence can be increased because you know healing is taking place. The more you notice the journey, the quicker you move out of the place of pain and damage, so be aware of how you're interacting with yourself and your surroundings. Even watching something may cause a step forward.

I was watching a DVD of a series I hadn't previously seen. In one of the episodes the main character related a saying I'd never heard before; 'if you meet an asshole in the morning, they're the asshole, but if you meet assholes all day, you're the asshole.' Not only did it make me smile, but I immediately related it to Lissa. She'd always had issues with other people, whether family, friends, work colleagues, customers, ex partners or even strangers, and in my mind I changed the saying to, 'if you have a problem with someone in the morning, they're the problem, but if you have problems with people all day, you're the problem.'

It was simple, but it was a step forward in relation to seeing that she was the problem, not other people. She was the one who always had issues with others, whether real, half-truths or lies. It's one of the main ways by which she casts herself in the role of victim, of being a vulnerable sheep that needs protecting by the rest of the flock. It was also one of the main ways by which she created my extrinsic focus. Now she was no longer in my life, it was starting to shift and the impact of that saying shows the reality was starting to sink in.

This shift first made itself known when I traversed a group of stepping stones on Saturday the 18th March and Sunday the 19th, two months after having left my mother's and just over four months since last contact with Lissa. On the Saturday morning I'd continued to have a series on which had been playing all the previous night. One of the characters mentioned the battle of Helms Deep, from *The Lord of the Rings* and I was taken by the urge to watch the trilogy. Lissa and I had watched them on a number of 'movie marathon' days, getting in snacks and snuggling together under a duvet on the three-seater in the lounge. Because of this, I fought the urge, sure that watching them would cause great upset.

However, early in the afternoon, I finally gave in and took the leap. Putting on *The Fellowship of the Ring*, I prepared for tears. Instead, I found myself smiling broadly when the title music came on and was pleasantly surprised.

Pressing 'play,' I watched it and found myself continuing to smile virtually all the way through, discovering that most of my thoughts related to my ex-wife. Those films had been far more special to us; we'd seen them at the cinema together, we'd had a minor *Lord of the Rings* theme at our wedding, which included one of the pieces of music from the first movie playing during the ceremony and a specially written poem speaking of two rings to unite our hearts. Just like Lissa and I, me and my ex-wife had watched the three films back-to-back on movie marathon days and I recalled all my ex-wife's favourite parts and the great impressions she used to do.

The only time I became sad was towards the end, when the hobbit Frodo hears the words of Gandalf the wizard, words which are quoted at the start of this book. The tears they induced didn't last long and I came away from that film feeling much stronger and brighter than I had in a long time.

I'd overcome the anticipated pain of watching the movie and it hadn't matched the reality. This caused me to realise that in at least some instances, the anticipation of how I'd react was stopping me from doing certain things. This didn't mean I then decided to watch films which had a very strong emotional link to Lissa, but it did mean that, on that Saturday night, no DVD played while I slept for the first time since arriving in Scotland.

When I woke on the settee on Sunday morning, I got up, fed the cats and made my first coffee. I was sitting drinking it in the utility room while blowing the smoke of my cigarettes out of the cat flap when I realised I had yet to think of Lissa. There was a mix of amazement and relief. For the first time in memory, she hadn't been my first thought. It was an important stepping stone and another followed that same day; I didn't play any DVD's until the evening. When I did, it was to continue with *The Lord of the Rings* trilogy and once more no DVD played through the night. As it turned out, that loop had been broken. Though there were still odd occasions when I needed something on to distract my mind as I went to sleep, on the whole the TV and DVD were turned off.

That weekend was significant. Things were changing. I was becoming comfortable with silence, which showed the intensity of the thoughts and emotions was starting to fade, at least for the most part. The extrinsic focus was beginning to lose its hold and I was gaining greater liberty from the impacts of Lissa's abuse.

This was helped by turning some of my attention to the back garden. This began in a small way not long after my arrival at the new house. I began to feed bread to the birds, as I'd done on a daily basis in Cornwall. When my first online grocery delivery arrived, I filled a bird feeder my mother had given me for Christmas with feed I'd ordered and hung it from the silver birch in the middle of the garden. Initially, there was no joy in providing the sustenance, it was simply done out of my wish to help the local wildlife.

However, as the house became a home, I found myself spending more time thinking about what I wanted to do in order to make my garden a haven for wildlife and help support biodiversity. In late March, I created a bluebell and wildflower area in one corner, buying 60 of the former and scattering hundreds of wildflower seeds. I also bought and planted a plum tree and a number of fruit bushes.

Then, in mid-April, I dug out a small pond in the middle of the garden, buying plants to go in it and using the earth to create contouring along one edge, which was then planted with wildflower seeds. There were other touches too, like finding an old coal scuttle and planting a beautiful azalea bush in it. One of the most recent things I did was plant fluffy white flowers in an old pair of DMs I had. This was a significant stepping stone and happened in mid-May.

The boots had lasted 20 years before they'd been retired from active service. That retirement had occurred a few years previous and yet I'd not used them as planters in Cornwall despite having the idea while living there. It was as if I knew I wouldn't be staying. Moreover, the fact I'd now used them in that way in Scotland was a hint in regards how I was feeling about my new location, but more of that later.

These activities in the garden were stepping stones. They indicated that the extrinsic focus Lissa had caused was losing its hold. Though I was often thinking of her while out there, there were also many occasions when I wasn't. This was further strengthened by engaging in nature photography to increasing degrees, something which has long been a hobby of mine. When I was looking for or taking a shot, I was absorbed by the activity, almost becoming one with the subject, and there were no thoughts of Lissa.

It is also important to note that study after study has shown nature promotes calmness and psychological wellbeing. Even urban greenery has been shown to reduce heart rate and anxiety, along with improving attention and mood. In this light, it should come as no surprise I found myself out in the garden more and more, especially as I was creating a wild garden, and so had untamed nature right outside my back door. So, when you get the chance, spend some time in the wilds, in your garden, your yard or local parkland. It will help and there'll likely be things which can help distract you from incessant thoughts about what's happened. Seek nature's embrace. Let it quiet your mind and sow the seeds of happiness.

Remember, stepping stones can be subtle or obvious. They can offer hints as to your recovery or be massive great signs showing you with flashing neon lights. Whatever form they take, you will find yourself standing on new ones as you heal.

Keep an eye out for them. If friends and family mention you're getting stronger, but you're unsure, ask them how they know. Build your confidence on the journey of recovery, because you are recovering and you will heal. Say after me and with a nod; 'I *will* heal.'

Chapter Nine

Writing it Down, Talking it Out

Writing down your thoughts and feelings can really help. The same is true of expressing them verbally. Both serve to alleviate internal pressure. It's also the case that seeing or hearing what's been previously trapped in your head may provide new insights. These ways of expressing yourself are both a release valve and a way to explore how you're feeling. Writing and/or talking about the abuse can be calming, revealing or simply help you free the words that are otherwise endlessly circling your mind.

When mine and Lissa's relationship as a couple came to an end in July 2021, I found myself writing my thoughts in a notebook. These would go from positive to negative and back again, depending upon my mood. They were a coping mechanism in light of the emotional pain I was going through. They also served to highlight how different my thoughts were depending on my state of mind, something which showed me that it's important to sleep, eat and not take any action when in an agitated state. States change and it's much better to make decisions when calm and collected.

When Lissa went to the Greek island in spring 2022, I bought another notepad. I found that I needed to write down my thoughts once again as I struggled to cope with the diminished contact and then with the change in her treatment of me. This, like the previous occasion, was a coping mechanism.

It helped to write things down in a couple of ways. The first was the release of pressure, as mentioned. Rather than letting the thoughts circle, I tried to expel them onto the paper and cage them in ink. This wasn't always successful, but there was definitely an easing of the intensity of my feelings. I also doubt whether it makes a difference whether you write by hand or straight onto an electronic device, like a laptop, so do what you're most comfortable with. What's more, there's no need to read over what you've written. This is a way to expel your pain and confusion and, once the words are expelled, you can simply leave them unread. It may be that once you've healed, you throw any notepads relating to your trauma away or burn them. The latter can be especially powerful and I'll speak about it in Chapter Fifteen: *Happiness*.

The second way in which writing things down helped was by giving me the ability to read what I'd written. As I said in the previous paragraph, this isn't necessary, but I found it useful. This is because I'd written certain insights and phrases in bold and underlined them. This meant I could easily look back through the notepads in order to remind myself of what I'd come to realise or understand.

Both notebooks were like thought diaries. Though I didn't write in them every day, it was often and it's possible to chart my changing mentality and mood. It's also clear that, deep down, I knew Lissa was all about Lissa. I'd noted her self-obsession and need for attention, but was struggling to accept these aspects of who she is. However, I had no idea about her pathological lying or use of narcissistic mixed messages at either time. She's so good at concealing this that, if fate hadn't intervened, I probably wouldn't have found out the truth of who she is or that I'd been abused the entire time.

Writing *The Gentle Man and the Butterfly* was not part of the healing process. It was my attempt to preserve and present what I'd thought was a wonderful period of my life. It was also sadly part of the discovery process, bringing to light some horrific behaviour on her part, including the two that had the biggest impact on me. They were like atomic bombs levelling all I thought we'd shared and who I thought she was. I was completely lost in the maelstrom of thoughts and emotions they caused. Every thought, every emotion and every waking moment of every day was tainted by the radiation of everything she'd done and all the things that potentially still remained unknown to me. I was sickened by it on every level and there were many times when I didn't think I could take any more.

Then there was the clash of what had been discovered with who I thought she was and what I thought we'd shared. To use another metaphor; it was like metal grinding against metal, neither giving way, but filling me with painful sparks and unbearable screeching as I tried to make them fit together.

On the other hand, writing *Life After Mental Abuse* has been part of my recovery. It has helped me come to terms with what has happened and also to see how far I've come in the months since first writing notes for this book in mid-February. When I looked back at these in early April, I found they primarily related to Lissa, the extrinsic focus still apparent. When I discovered this, I started to make a conscious effort to make this book about me, about the impact of the abuse on my mental and emotional states, and about my recovery process. I'd already written our story, in which I'd focussed on her and 'us.' This book, on the other hand, is my story.

Life After Mental Abuse isn't the only writing I've been engaged in as part of my healing. I've also written poems and a piece of prose. The latter, along with a selection of the former is included in Appendix I in order to show other possible avenues to express yourself in the written word. There's quite a few and if you feel drawn to writing about how you're feeling, then chose the form or forms that suit you best. Experiment if you want. Try a few ways and be both open and honest in the moment. Just let it out and let yourself find at least some small sense of release.

When it comes to talking it out, I'm quite lucky (as I am in regards writing considering I've been an author for many years). This is because I find it easy to speak about my thoughts and emotions. I'm a very chatty man and enjoy good conversation. I'm also very open about myself, my life, my thoughts and my feelings. This means that, when I'm in emotionally charged states, such as being overcome with love, joy, excitement or distress, I often become even more expressive, barely able to hold in my emotions. This was the case when Lissa's treatment of me began to decline.

By this point, I was already exhibiting extrinsic focus. Though I was unaware of it, my mother had seen it plainly when I stayed with her for Christmas 2021, later stating that she hadn't recognised her son. Because I was virtually totally focused on Lissa, the change of treatment had even greater impact than would have otherwise been the case. It caused a vast amount of confusion due to having no idea why it was taking place, what had changed or what was truly happening on the Greek island. It also caused heartache, angst, agitation and restlessness. I was unable to function properly, but spent every waking hour trying to work out what was going on while also trying to keep upbeat, light, supportive and playful in my messages to her. This was done so she wouldn't be negatively affected by how I was feeling, to keep her as stable as I could and in the hope the Lissa I knew and loved would return.

There were glimpses of the woman I'd known, but they were increasingly fleeting. After a few days of being cold and unaffectionate, she'd suddenly send a bright and loving message. I held on to these as a drowning man holds onto a piece of rotting timber, trying to convince myself that the waters would calm and I'd once more find myself sailing on the ocean of what we'd shared.

At the same time, I talked out all the questions and puzzles that plagued me with Sandi, Cheryl (called Chelsea in *The Gentle Man and the Butterfly*) and my mother. Whenever I'd meet Sandi for a walk or head to Cheryl's for a coffee and catch up, the conversation would be dominated by anxieties, concerns and hurt in relation to how Lissa was behaving. I simply couldn't stop myself. After a few of the walks with Sandi, I even told myself that next time I'd make every effort not to talk about the situation, but it was to no avail. Why? I needed to let it out, to release all the thoughts and emotions that were swirling around inside.

This continued beyond the end of our contact. While living with my mother, she became the primary source of release. I didn't necessarily need a response, I just needed to get the thoughts out in order to ease the pressure. Essentially, I needed someone to listen as all the pain and confusion came tumbling out, often accompanied by tears.

Though it didn't always feel like it helped, it did. Talking out everything I was going through not only lessened the internal pressure of it all, but also sometimes provided me with insight, just like writing things down. I'd hear myself say something and would be struck by a new revelation or a new angle.

I'd also be given opinions by the people I was speaking to. They often felt like I wasn't listening to their comments relating to Lissa's true nature, but they were slowly sinking in. So, if you're a friend or family member of someone who's suffering or suffered from abuse, don't despair if your observations seem to be having no impact. It can take a while for victims to reach a place where they can accept what's happened and what someone they cared for has done to them, but your comments do help and will give them additional strength in the long run. When I started to see the truth, I would remember what Cheryl and others had said to me, and their words helped to cement the reality of who Lissa is and the abuse she'd carried out.

Talking about it was a vital part of dealing with Lissa's increasingly open mistreatment and then became a vital part of recovery, which came to include therapy. Talking to those closest to me and my therapist allowed me to see through the illusion of who I thought Lissa was and come to terms with the reality. It allowed me to see what was happening in me and why I was struggling to let certain things go. It also highlighted the need for much greater awareness of mixed messages.

I recall Cheryl saying on more than one occasion during the unexplained decline in Lissa's treatment of me that it seemed I was obsessed with her. If either of us had known of mixed messages, we'd have realised this was a sign of being a victim of mental abuse. Further, we'd have understood I was exhibiting the symptoms of extrinsic focus and confused agitation, rather than being obsessed.

In all, I found talking about the situation easy. In fact, it would have been more difficult not to, something underlined by my failure to stop talking about it with Sandi. I was in an extremely heightened mental and emotional state and it was centred entirely on Lissa.

I understand some do not find it as easy to talk about what's going on inside their hearts and minds, but try and find a way. Approach a friend or family member and simply be honest with them, tell them you need someone to listen so you can let it out and no longer feel like you may explode from the build-up of internal pressure. If you have no one close you feel you can speak to, find a therapist.

It may sound strange, but you can even talk to your pets or plants. They may not understand the words, but they know the emotions present and the important thing is you're expressing yourself. I've spoken to my cats a couple of times and I've even apologised to my houseplants for the negative atmosphere on bad days. You never know, talking in this way may lead to you gaining the courage to talk to a friend.

There are also phone lines you can ring, such as the Samaritans, along with organisations specifically related to mental abuse. Some of these are listed in Appendix III: *Useful Contacts*. You're also welcome to contact me if you have the feeling you want to get in touch and the two possible ways to do so are also listed in that section.

Whoever you do it with, talking out what's happening or has happened to you is an effective way of helping ease the situation, come to terms with it and to arrive at new perspectives. It's a way to gain greater clarity and insights from those you're talking to. This can be especially effective if they're friends or family who know about the relationship in question.

There's a new word I discovered while writing this book; exulansis. It means giving up trying to talk about an experience because others can't relate to it. Don't give in to this feeling. I know it can occur because I felt it in relation to a number of people who clearly didn't understand. I chose not to speak with them about the events any more and thereby avoid any frustration or sense of defeat. Instead, I continued to talk to those who, even if they didn't fully grasp the affects of the mental abuse, were empathetic.

Don't be afraid to be emotional when you're writing it down or talking it out. Don't be scared about expressing love, yearning, heartache, frustration, anger, hate, fear, anxiety or any other feelings, no matter if you're concerned others may find them foolish. Talking it out isn't about what others think, it's primarily about you expressing the turmoil within to lessen its intensity.

I regularly mentioned how much I still loved Lissa and many of those times felt the other person would think I was crazy after everything that had happened. If I felt I could, I'd hesitantly mention that I still hoped maybe she'd end up living with me in Scotland one day in order to genuinely undergo therapy with me at her side. I was hesitant because I knew what the reaction would be to such a statement, but I needed to express it.

Talking about the situation doesn't just involve letting out things like an overwhelming sense of betrayal, it also means letting out such things as a heartfelt wish for the other's return. Both have to end and one of the ways to help bring about their demise is to release them in words. It's like taking away some of their power. While you hold them inside, they remain strong and linger. When you put voice to them, some of their vigour is lost, even if you don't notice at the time. I didn't realise this and, if I had, I'd have explained to my friends so that they would understand I was actually in the process of letting go of both the hardship and the unrealistic and ultimately unhealthy wishes for Lissa to return into my life.

Speaking it out allows you to hear your own thoughts, drawing them out of the tangle in your head. Helping you untangle them is part of what a therapist does and it's time to talk about this useful tool in coping with the aftermath of abuse.

Chapter Ten

Therapy

Four months after last hearing from Lissa and nearly two months after moving into the property in Scotland, I put the post on LinkedIn regarding *The Gentle Man and the Butterfly, Volume 1: The Light Rises*. It was this which caused me to realise I needed professional help, as I mentioned in Chapter Three.

One of my contacts on there is an American woman who was friends with Lissa when she did her work placement on the Greek island. When our contact had initially come to an end in September 2022, I'd contacted the woman in the hope of finding out the truth about Lissa's time there, certain she'd kept a number of things hidden from me. Rather than informing me of what had actually happened, she told Lissa I'd been in touch, something which led to the brief reestablishment of our contact. I understand why she did so despite not having been in contact with Lissa for some time. After all, I was a stranger and the idea that Lissa could be deceiving people is at odds with the persona she presents to the world.

The attempt to uncover more of the truth had led to the American being one of my connections on LinkedIn and her past behaviour suggested she may let Lissa know about the books. This led to a state of extreme anxiety after posting on the site. It felt like I'd made no progress, my mental and emotional state exactly the same as when I used to wait for her responses in the last few months of our contact. I was restless, tense and agitated. I barely slept and, when I woke very early in the morning, I immediately deleted the post. However, the anxiety didn't simply vanish, but continued for many hours, slowly fading as time passed.

It was this reaction and its similarity to the way I'd felt when we were in the final throes of our contact which caused me to realise I was far from over the abuse. Even the merest possibility of hearing from her had sent me straight back to the way I'd felt months before. Though there had been positive changes in other areas, there had been no change in that regard.

The obviousness of the anxiety and the degree to which it had been felt caused me to contact a local psychotherapist that very morning. In our preliminary chat, which lasted 30-40 minutes, she was already recognising that Lissa was abusive and had been highly manipulative.

To hear those things from a mental health professional brought with it a kind of calm. My friends and family had been saying the same things, some for a considerable amount of time. However, I was well aware that those closest to me were likely to be protective and their opinions may be coloured by that fact. To have someone totally independent confirm what they'd been saying, someone who was trained in the field of mental health, brought a level of confirmation that caused the idea of Lissa being my abuser to take hold to a greater degree after having fought the idea for so long.

I fought it for a couple of reasons. The first was simple; I loved her. The second was due to not wanting to accept she'd treated me that way, that she'd in fact been calculating and controlling rather than in love with me. It was a painful thing to accept, especially in light of how I felt about our time together. I couldn't comprehend how she could have seen it so differently, had been totally convinced she wanted to be with me and had appreciated our life together. The clash of what I'd thought and the reality of the situation had been a constant source of distress. The therapy would help alleviate this distress, causing me to become increasingly aware that her experience of the relationship and friendship that followed wasn't remotely comparable to mine.

Due to the therapist encouraging me to start focussing on my feelings rather than Lissa's, I started to see more clearly just how she'd become the centre of my existence. Again, a professional voicing such things makes a difference. Friends and family have your best interests at heart, but I knew mine viewed Lissa in an extremely negative light. I didn't and my continuing feelings for her made me yearn to help her, as I'd done many times during the time she was in my life. I knew she wasn't aware of some of her symptoms, but that she understood she had serious issues. I wanted to be there to encourage and support her, and to provide any insight I thought may be useful. Part of the reason I chose to publish the books was so that I could communicate with her, seeing no other way of doing so. In fact, writing them had helped maintain my focus on her, spending almost three months totally immersed in thoughts of her, our life together, all the good times we'd shared, all the hopes for the future I'd had and all the terrible things she'd done.

There's no escaping the fact that this book also has an element of that, of making myself look back to much darker times, which can sometimes be hard. However, this act of charting the impact and recovery is important so that others can be helped, encouraged and enlightened.

Before beginning therapy, I thought I was too different in lifestyle and looks to be loved. I was too sensitive for this world. I was too loving, trusting and forgiving. Time and again, I was critical of who I am. I also chastised myself for having been fooled and used for so long. This further undermined my self-esteem and self-confidence, making me feel as though I was ill-suited to interact with other members of my species because I was clearly flawed as a person.

I was wrong, but needed another shift of perspective to see this and, once more, it had to be coupled with acceptance. In this instance, the shift happened thanks to therapy. I was seeing myself as the problem when the truth was that Lissa was the problem. She'd taken advantage of me, but that didn't mean my qualities were somehow negative or made me a lesser human being. It meant she didn't value me as she should.

Being subjected to sustained and sometimes sadistic abuse by someone you love is not an easy thing to accept or deal with, especially when you didn't suspect a thing until so late in the day. There's an element of shock involved, adding to the psychological trauma. This, coupled with the abuse itself, meant there were some emotionally charged issues to be worked through.

My decision to seek therapy is one of the best I've taken on the road to recovery. Some may not feel it's necessary or right for them, and that's what I thought for a time.

Before that initial call with the therapist, I had no idea how much difference it could make just having confirmation from a professional about the role Lissa had played. Since then, I've gained greater insight in regards myself and my motivations for trying to cling onto what I'd felt Lissa and I had shared. This is partly thanks to a good rapport with my therapist, which is vitally important. Also vitally important is being totally open and honest with both yourself and the therapist. There's no point undertaking therapy if you're not willing to be that way.

I'd recommend therapy to anyone who's suffered from mental abuse. Even if you don't feel you need it, you may be surprised. The day before seeking out a therapist, I would have stated with confidence that I had no need of one, believing myself to be well on the way to healing. The post on LinkedIn proved otherwise in a very dramatic way.

Don't wait for something like that. Ring around and talk to a few therapists until you find one with whom you feel comfortable. If the first session shows there's no rapport, don't be afraid to find another. You need a good patient-therapist relationship to develop in order to deal with the very hard things which you've been put through, and they *will* help you deal with them. There needs to be a bond of trust so you can allow yourself to be vulnerable and raw.

When it comes to mine, she understood my wish not to be seen out in public and our sessions were conducted over the internet via Zoom. Up until some point in April, I was seated in a shadowy corner, not wanting to be seen clearly. Then, after some important changes in acceptance, not only of the situation, but of myself, I swapped seats, sitting directly before the phone and in full daylight. This change was immediately noted and, from that appointment until our last session, there were even smiles and laughter.

I chose when the therapy began and when it came to an end. I knew I was ready to finish, was in a very different place compared to when it had begun. This book was nearing its completion and in itself had become an act of letting go. Upon its release, I would be releasing Lissa. With this in mind and aware of how much stronger I was, the last therapy session occurred in mid-May, shortly before completing *Life After Mental Abuse*.

You have control of how many sessions you have and, if you have the right therapist, also on how they are conducted. They may ask if you feel like undertaking certain exercises and, even if they seem a little strange, I'd also advise trying to push yourself to do them. This can involve role play and the use of your imagination, and it's important you throw yourself into them. From those I did, I can attest to how powerful and cathartic they can be.

The simple golden rule of therapy is that you are totally open and honest. Try not to doctor or mediate your thoughts and emotions, but express them without edit. It's important the therapist knows what's happening within you if they're truly going to help, and they really can help. I can't express how grateful I am to mine. I'm also grateful for having her to talk to at a time when I was starting to feel guilty about unloading on my mother, Cheryl and Sandi. They'd already taken so much and this was all but brought to an end as I underwent therapy. Knowing I'd be able to discuss things with my therapist meant I didn't need to do so with anyone else to a great extent.

So, this gives you another option. Whether you take it or not, you will still continue to heal. Recovery still happens and only you can know if you're in need of extra assistance.

Chapter Eleven

Changing Focus

This chapter concerns another set of loops, ones which went beyond the impact of the abuse. These loops were of thoughts about Lissa. They were varied in themselves and included an attempt to understand how she could have treated me so badly, a sense of injustice that she continued to live her life as if she'd done nothing wrong, a hope that she'd seek help and worry that she wouldn't, a continuing wish to have contact with her and a continuing belief that she was meant to join me in Scotland.

All these loops were part of extrinsic focus and, despite how many times friends and family members told me I needed to focus on myself, I simply couldn't break free. She had been the most important person in my life for over four years, something strengthened by the persona she presents and playing the victim, so it's only natural these loops existed. They were added to by the fact I was trying to square who I thought she was with who she really was.

I'd had more happy times, more physically intimate times and more great experiences with Lissa than with anyone else. Physically, mentally and emotionally, I felt closer to her than I thought possible. More, she silenced my deep-rooted feeling of isolation and difference, something which no one else had come close to doing. I felt fulfilled and complete when I was with Lissa.

The only place I'd ever felt like I belonged was western Cornwall but, for the first time, I truly felt like I belonged with someone, with her. To discover this was all one-way, that she had never really felt the same, was heartbreaking and hard to comprehend.

How could such a strong love develop based on illusion? I simply couldn't grasp it and so couldn't let go of the idea that she had two distinct sides, one light and the other dark. This created a kind of excuse for her actions because she couldn't help what she'd done when the dark side was in control. It allowed me to continue thinking the light side of her had cared deeply for me. My love and compassion for her, both of which are very evident in *The Gentle Man and the Butterfly*, meant that letting go of the hope it had all somehow been real was a very hard thing to do.

Along with pining and yearning, there was also sometimes a sense of injustice. I was enduring intense emotional trauma and yet she got to go on regardless. If she'd have physically abused me for such a sustained period of time and to such a severe degree, she would likely be in prison but, as it was, was able to go about her life as if she'd done nothing wrong.

This sense of injustice also meant I sometimes had to fight the urge to send copies of the books to her parents. None of her family had any real idea what role I'd played in her life and may not have even known we were a couple, but instead were under the impression I'd simply been her landlord. I knew for certain they had no idea we'd been engaged. I felt that I deserved them to know the truth and that they deserved to know as well, especially as she often used them to strengthen the appearance of being a victim.

On other occasions, I wanted her family to know in order to help her. At those times I had to fight the urge to contact her sister-in-law. From what I'd gleaned, she seemed the most likely to have a compassionate response and would get the family to approach the matter carefully and with kindness when confronting Lissa, hopefully helping her to genuinely seek therapy and change.

The swing from positive to negative thoughts was hard to deal with, especially as love still remained the driving force behind both. I kept telling myself I needed to let go, but as I looked out across the Irish Sea in the direction of Belfast, my mind couldn't help but turn to her. The house had been bought to be closer to her and that was something which caused a lot of pain. I was closer, but she was more out of reach than at any time before.

The trauma persisted, but so did the improvement. There would be a good week, even two. Then, without warning, there'd be an absolutely terrible day when all I wanted was to escape the pain. I'd sleep as much as possible, hoping I'd wake to find it gone. I even remember curling up on the cool floor of the utility room on one occasion early during my recovery, wishing it wall all simply go away and I'd wake to find my heart and mind free of the weight I carried.

If the good, bad and mixed days had been plotted on a graph, you'd have seen change was taking place, but it was slow. It takes time and isn't a constant upward movement. You can think your tears are all done and then the smallest thing can set you off again. On a day when I was struggling, just seeing a butterfly flit through my garden caused me to break down due to its connection with Lissa and the important symbolism we'd associated with the beautiful insects. On a good day, that same butterfly may gave brought a smile or even chuckle as it brought to mid happy memories of us together as a couple or, supposedly, best friends.

Lissa had been and remained my primary focus. I thought about what we'd had and what we'd lost. I thought about what she'd done and what she was doing. I considered the likelihood that I'd never spend time in her company again, never see her smile, hear her laugh or sing, have a conversation or share a meal. I couldn't bear the thought of never holding her again. And I was torn apart by the thought of the isolation I now felt more keenly than ever before remaining for the rest of my life if fate didn't somehow bring her back to me.

This last was a prominent part of the pain. I felt so alone after having experienced the belonging of being with her, even as friends. Helping to compound this feeling was the fact I'd moved hundreds of miles from my close friends. It didn't help that this had been done for her and us.

There were two elements that were important in breaking the extrinsic focus. The first was the wish for Lissa to return. In spite of the mental and emotional trauma she'd caused, I still wanted her back during the early months of recovery. Part of me hoped she'd read the books and realise just how special our relationship had been, along with how much she needed to seek help. I hoped she'd come to me, wanting to reignite what we'd had as a couple and for me to support her through treatment. The reality, of course, was that even knowing I'd published the books would likely make her angry and hateful as I'd revealed who she really is to anyone who read them.

That was the second element which was important in changing my focus; accepting the reality of who she is and what she'd done. I clearly hadn't accepted that she had intentionally and knowingly abused me. I hadn't accepted that she'd likely used me the entire time and had never felt any love for me. And I couldn't bring myself to accept that her behaviour reflected who she really is, not some dark side, some shadow self. My heart wanted to cling onto the idea that the feelings I had for her and our life had been mutual. I wasn't able to accept that only my feelings had been real.

It's always been hard for me to let go of precious times in my life. As a boy, I'd often cry myself to sleep after a particularly good day, realising it was lost and could never be experienced again. On those occasions, my mother had tried to comfort me and, even as a man, I struggle to release times which have been special. This meant it was that much harder to let go of my time with Lissa as I still viewed it as predominantly good.

However, I began to retrain my brain, using some of the things she'd done to help bring about change in the way I thought about what we'd had. I also reminded myself of the realities at times when I wished for her return. For example, every time I wished she'd arrive at the house, her car packed with belongings and with the earnest desire to be with me once more, I'd remind myself she'd never wanted to be with me in the first place, that it was utterly unrealistic. I'd tell myself that, though my feelings had been real, hers had been false. I'd bring to mind what she'd done, seeing the abuse and manipulation.

The more I reminded myself of such things, the more the wish for her return faded. Instead, the reality of the situation gently took its place. There was angst, heartache and tears as I released that hope. I knew it wasn't healthy, that it put my future firmly in the hands of something that had never really existed. I had to let it go. I had to let her go. And I had to let the illusion of both go. I had to face reality. That was the only way forward. There was no real choice but to look to a life without her. That was a big step in changing my focus from her to me and my life, one which was helped by my therapist.

Thanks in part to her insightful comments, I started to plainly see that I was still extrinsically focussed. I was still talking about wanting to help and support Lissa, about what she was doing, how she was and my concerns for her long-term happiness, expressing the hope she'd seek help. Once I saw this, things changed. I began to shut down such thoughts and instead try and think about how I was doing, what I wanted to do that day and where my life was going.

Slowly but surely, such thoughts of Lissa became less frequent. I became increasingly focussed on my own healing, on rebuilding my self-esteem and self-acceptance, and seeing to my mental and emotional wellbeing in general. I started to emerge from the cocoon, the thoughts of her which had wrapped themselves tightly about my mind finally beginning to fall away. When I did think about her, those thoughts were commonly about what she'd done and I came to see there was no shadow self. I saw her with increased clarity and understood there was no excuse for what she'd done, that she'd consciously chosen to behave in such ways.

It was this change that caused me to decide to use Lissa's real first name. This happened in April and, until that point, the manuscript was a mix of Lucy and Lissa. When I was still clinging onto the hope what we'd had was real, that she had cared for me and her behaviour was unintentional, caused by the shadow self I imagined her to have, I'd use Lucy. When I could see the truth of the situation, I'd use Lissa. Once the truth settled, it became my only choice, one which was welcomed by others because it showed I was taking ownership of what had happened.

It could be that my choice to use Lucy in *The Gentle Man and the Butterfly* not only showed I hadn't accepted the truth, but also helped cement the idea of two separate identities. I've thought about going back and changing it to Lissa, but have chosen to leave it true to the time.

Another event which relates to *The Gentle Man and the Butterfly* occurred on 10th April. I realised that, though I couldn't publish it in a single paperback volume because of its length, I could do so as a Kindle exclusive ebook edition. Due to my growing strength and acceptance, I published it as *The Complete Story* and, most importantly, released it under my name rather than anonymously. This helped increase my sense of growing strength. It also showed I was accepting the truth of what had happened and that both my perspective and focus were changing.

If you're focussed on your abuser or on what happened, try to break its hold. Turn your focus on yourself. It's you who's been wounded and needs to heal. Try and note when your focus shifts to them or events relating to them. When it does, find ways to bring it back to you and the present. How are you feeling? What do you hope to do that day? Where do you see yourself in a week, a month, a year?

If you're a friend or family member, gently point out when the victim's focus is locked on the abuser or the relationship they'd had. Ask them about themselves, about their responses to such thoughts. That can help turn their considerations from the past to their own state of heart and mind. It's soft encouragement to alter their focus and, given time, this will happen.

From what I've related above, it's clear that a change in focus went hand in hand with growing acceptance. The more I accepted the role Lissa played and what she'd done, the less inclined I was to have thoughts about her well being, return or to consider how much I missed her. This decrease, along with the encouragement of others to focus on myself, caused me to start putting myself back together rather than worrying about trying to support and help her. Thankfully, once the extrinsic focus was all but broken, that process became relatively easy, especially once I'd truly faced the realities.

Chapter Twelve

Acceptance

Accepting you've been abused can be hard and when your abuser is someone you trusted, respected and loved, that process is even harder. It took me quite some time until I could acknowledge Lissa had mentally abused me, partly because this would cast the woman I loved in the role of 'abuser.' I couldn't reconcile the one with the other, couldn't believe she could be both the love of my life and my abuser.

This remained the case during the final months of our contact when she was openly abusive. It also continued for a long time afterwards and, even when I first started therapy, I would defend Lissa and make excuses for her, such as her abusive behaviour being related to past traumas.

As the recovery process continued, my perspectives began to shift and change. This was an important part of the healing process and with it came ever greater acceptance.

I came to understand that her treatment of me had always been a matter of choice. No matter what trauma she may or may not have suffered in the past, she had chosen to be abusive and that abuse had been present from the start. There was no getting away from the fact she'd willingly chosen to lie and manipulate, to calculate, control, cheat and be cruel. It was those choices which have led to the creation of this book and moulded the content of *The Gentle Man and the Butterfly* to a large degree.

I also came to accept that the idea our story would break through to her and she'd realise she needed to change was a flight of fancy, as was the connected hope that she'd come to realise how special our relationship was and that she loved me. Despite agreeing to marry me and stating that she loved me for the entire four years, it had already become apparent that Lissa's supposed affection was likely false. In fact, it seemed she may not have even particularly cared about me, that I'd merely been a means to an end. This was devastating and its impact was initially felt about halfway through the stay at my mother's. The ground, which had already been crumbing, suddenly fell away from under my feet. I was left in freefall surrounded by darkness.

It had a severe effect on my self-esteem, making me feel as though I was unlovable. As previously mentioned, I also couldn't understand how I'd come to love her more than any other if her feelings had been counterfeit. How could such deep affection be inspired by false pretences? I wrestled with this for a long time, thinking that surely I must somehow be wrong, that she must have had genuine affection for mine to be so powerful.

Ultimately, I had to concede that, though my feelings had been real, hers had not. I spent four years under the impression she loved me as a partner and then as her best friend. Now, I don't think I was ever really either of these things to her. I was useful and that's all there was to it.

The struggle to deal with this mentally and emotionally contributed a great deal to my mental state in the early weeks of my life in Scotland. It was such a painful part of what had been revealed that it took longer to accept than many other aspects of what she'd done and how she'd treated me.

The acceptance of the above changed how I viewed our time together. All the brightness I'd once seen in the four years drained away. My chest tight as I bent double and rocked back and forth, I shed a great many tears and felt a profound sense of loss. The last element I'd been clinging onto had been released. I'd accepted the darkness behind those memories and with that the final light of our time together had gone out.

It was a sad result of coming to terms with everything and it was down to Lissa. It felt like she'd stolen all the goodness and replaced it with a sense of being deceived and betrayed. Even at times when we were alone and enjoying nature, she was living other lives beside the one we had. What had once been so precious existed only as the love I still felt for her, but even that was a wilting rose, its thorns digging deep.

Remember the mid-map of the village of my life? If you recall, I had a memorial garden for all the good times we'd shared and the smiling face of Lissa had been placed there. When the goodness drained away, all the bright flowers and beautiful plants withered and died. The smile cracked and beneath was revealed parched earth. With acceptance, the garden became a barren graveyard beyond the outskirts of my internal village, no longer visited and instead left to a tangled growth of bare thorny vines.

Part of the reason I struggled to let go and accept what she'd done was because I wanted what we'd shared to be real. My heart ached for it to have been as I'd once seen it but, with my acceptance, the truth finally sank in.

This makes acceptance a double-edged sword. It's necessary in order to heal, but can bring its own pain. It can undo things which were precious to you and thereby have a strong emotional impact, one which was witnessed by my therapist on a number of occasions as I began to wake up to the realities.

Be prepared for tears. Be aware that they're part of the process of acknowledging the trauma and its cause. Be kind to yourself and appreciate each step you take towards owning the truth. Until you do, you can't move on.

It's also the case that acceptance isn't merely a chapter. Like other elements discussed, it's an ongoing part of the process which includes the acceptance of who you are. That's a really important step to take. You've got to start caring for and loving yourself again. It may be hard at first, but you can learn to embrace who you are.

You may feel foolish or embarrassed in the wake of what's happened. I certainly did on occasion. This was because of the obviousness of Lissa's abuse and manipulation in some instances, but it was only obvious in hindsight and after I'd accepted the reality of what had been going on. At the time, I was blinded to it, and it may be you were blinded to at least some of the abuse you underwent.

Friends and family may have been pointing it out to me, but I couldn't see it, at least not initially. I was blinded by love and the persona Lissa projects. You could picture me as a game show contestant and my family and friends as the audience. The charming, smiling and apparently loving host was making statements and the audience were shouting out which were true or false. Beneath the glare of the spotlights and intensity of the host's presence, I couldn't understand what they were saying. My heart and mind were so focussed on the host that nothing else mattered or could penetrate the wall of extrinsic focus. I wasn't foolish, I was being manipulated. The same is true of you. Let any such thoughts go.

Don't blame yourself. Nothing you have done led to you deserving to be treated in such a way. *They* were the problem, *not* you. You know what I'm going to ask you to do now, don't you? Repeat after me and nod; 'I was *never* the problem. *They* were the problem.' And that's the truth.

There is no justification for such treatment. They may attempt to transfer blame, but the blame lies solely at their feet. They chose to be abusive. You didn't ask them to treat you in such a way. How can you be blamed for something you had no say in and little or no knowledge of? They were responsible for their words and deeds, and they were in control.

Let go of anything they said or did that was intended to undermine you. That's all it was; a tactic by which to destabilise your sense of self. It wasn't based on anything real. Your abuser targeted your weak points, such as an element of how you look or who you are that you don't particularly like. They purposefully knocked your confidence in order to undermine you, making it easier to manipulate and control. That was the motivation behind such abuse. They weren't expressing the truth, they were essentially acting like a bully. It's not a reflection of any aspect of you. It's actually a refection of their aggressive personality and such things as a lack of empathy or moral boundaries. They are the one with issues, not you. Again, *they* were the problem, *not* you.

Remember, their abuse was self-motivated and self-serving. It wasn't because of anything you did. Let go of any embarrassment or sense of foolishness. Let go of any thoughts of blame. Let go of any negative views of yourself they contrived to create or reinforce. Don't let the affect of the abuser continue, that way they win. Fight back. See them and for who they truly are. See what they did as stemming from their own issues and release all the negative thoughts and feelings they've generated. They created them under false pretences and with only one motivation in mind; themselves.

Now they're no longer in your life, recognise and throw off the shackles of their abuse and revel in your liberty. I mean it, it's time to throw your hands in the air and wave them like you just don't give a damn what they said and did. It didn't relate to you, it related to them. They're pitiable and will always be locked in loneliness because they don't show themselves to anyone. Much of the attention they receive, whatever form its takes, isn't genuine, it's manipulated into existence. They will never be loved for who they are and won't ever find lasting happiness. But, hey, just look at you. You're a bundle of awesome potential who's got every chance of finding love and happiness. You're a better person. And, what's more, you're on the road to realising just how wonderful life can be without your abuser in it. Accept they were the problem and let them go.

Chapter Thirteen

Resurgence & Release

You will have times of calm, happiness and even joy, times of feeling like you've been released from a very dark and lonely prison, but be ready for the emotions and feelings you thought were over to re-emerge. Recovery isn't a smooth journey from point A to point B. There are ups and downs along the way and some may take you by surprise. Don't let them discourage you, they're just part of the process.

On 7th April, which was Good Friday, I had a terrible day after a couple of weeks of feeling progressively stronger. The tears kept coming time and again. I missed her. I struggled to understand how she could have treated me in such a way. I was angry with her. I loved her. All day long, I oscillated between various emotions and thoughts, ending up feeling drained and a little defeated after the good days which had gone before.

The following day, whatever it was that had caused the weight to press down on me again had lifted. Returning to a lesser degree on Easter Sunday, I then found it departing once more and haven't been so low since. However, I know it won't necessarily stay that way, to expect resurgences now and then.

I even had a glimpse back to the early weeks of living in Scotland on 1st May. I was tired and struggling, so decided to take some rest on the settee. I needed music to distract me because I'd been overcome by tears earlier that day, ones which had related to never seeing Lissa again and the likelihood she never had feelings for me.

Closing my eyes, I had thoughts the likes of which hadn't occurred in a long time. I imagined Lissa sneaking in through the back door, which was now usually unlocked during the daytime. She came into the lounge while I slept unawares and stabbed me in the chest.

The idea brought a touch of tension and the temptation to go and lock the door. Instead, I stayed put and let the images pass, both them and my response turning out to be fleeting. There'd been no evidence of such extreme imaginings for around two months by that point, so it was definitely unexpected.

The likely cause of the imagined attack was lack of sleep. This would have also contributed to my emotional state in the morning, making me more susceptible to being overcome by thoughts that wouldn't have had such a tearful impact on a day when I was well-rested and feeling stronger.

Getting a good night's sleep helps the recovery process. If sleep is minimal or disturbed, you're more likely to find yourself having strange or disrupted thought patterns. Thinking clearly and logically are both harder when tired, and levels of concentration drop. Memory can be affected and emotional states certainly are. You're more likely to be moody, low and lacking in motivation. Tears come more easily and the thoughts that bring them gain more power. This, considering the power of many of the thoughts during the impact and recovery processes, is the last thing you want to unintentionally add to.

There were a few occasions when I could feel myself getting progressively more tired over a particularly emotional period. Trying to deal with the impact of such intense trauma is exhausting in itself. Your brain is fried and yet, despite its circuits sparking and being in need of some necessary down time, you simply can't stop going over and over things. There's no 'off' switch. I know, I've looked. However, there are ways to artificially turn your brain off or at least distract it from those constant thoughts endlessly passing through its circuitry.

As you already know, I used DVD's playing repeatedly all night long as one means of finding sleep. This was clearly a distraction technique. Alternatively, you could listen to music or even talk radio. Anything that allows you to focus on something other than what's happening inside your head can help. Yes, thoughts still intrude and sometimes remain at the forefront, but at least it's not just them and the silence. It's the silence which can make them seem so loud. With other words and sounds in the background, their volume diminishes.

Another way I helped myself to sleep was mentioned in Chapter Seven: *Resisting Temptation*. On a handful of occasions, I used a small amount of alcohol to aid in relaxing me so I'd sleep better. I was confident that I wouldn't be tempted to get drunk and the drinks I had were very low volume, around 5%. Do not drink if you think you won't be able to stop. Do not drink if it's to get drunk. I've said it before and I'll say it again, alcohol is a depressant, and that's the last thing anyone recovering from mental abuse needs. A little is okay now and then, but that's it.

There's also another kind of drink which is good to limit, and that's coffee. Personally, I try and alternate between caffeinated and decaf in the day and have a 'cut-off point' of 5pm, after which I only have decaf. Caffeine is a stimulant, which means it increases the chance of not sleeping well or at all. Too much can also make you irritable and increase states of agitation you may be experiencing. I know people who have cut-off points earlier than mine and only you can know what effect it has, so create a cut-off point that's appropriate for you.

As well as drink, food helps with sleep. A good evening meal will mean your body is well fed and processing the food, often bringing a more drowsy state. It's also the case that you need to keep feeding yourself. That was one of the few things I was very aware of and managed to maintain during this entire time; the need to feed, but not in a *Lost Boys* kind of way, I assure you, that's what the abusers do.

Not eating reduces energy levels. Now, this may sound like it would be good as far as getting sleep goes, but it isn't. It, like lack of sleep, can intensify emotional states, cause 'fuzzy' thinking, lower your mood, add to the general lack of motivation and basically aid the negative states. By not eating or sleeping, you're actually lending the symptoms of abuse a hand in bringing you down. Instead, use these things to help with your recovery. The symptoms are powerful enough without your help, so help yourself instead.

You may need to do this with sleeping tablets, which is something I didn't use. I can't advise what kind to take as I'm not an expert. Nor is Google, so I'd advise seeing a healthcare professional to get advice. This said, I did use ibuprofen on a few occasions. Knowing that it makes me drowsy, I would take just one tablet in order to help induce sleep.

When it comes to the terrible state I was in on Good Friday, neither lack of sleep or food was to blame. It was simply part of dealing with such intense trauma. Imagine yourself climbing out of a deep well. The darkness is behind you and you're increasingly in the light. Your grip is becoming stronger and your progress easier. Every so often, echoes of your feelings when trapped at the bottom and scaling the walls below rise up to you because they have yet to fade away completely. They can cause you to feel as though you may slip and fall but, if you wait for them to pass, you'll find your upward journey continuing with increasing ease, possibly with shouts of encouragement from those closest to you. Maybe this book can even act as a ladder of sorts and help you heal with greater ease.

These resurgences are a natural part of recovery. If we return to 1st May, I started the day very emotionally, had the thought of Lissa stabbing me in the afternoon and then, in the early evening, something finally sank in that I'd been struggling with for a long time.

I sat in a window seat without a film on or any music playing. One of my cats was asleep on my lap as I watched the clouds and the sun went down. It was then that I finally accepted that Lissa had no shadow-self which was separate from her. She did it all, voluntarily, wilfully and in full knowledge of what she was doing. She did it all and there's no excuse.

That was an important place to get to, a vital acceptance, and shows that the brief resurgence of my fear and paranoia in the afternoon was just an echo rising up. There may be more resurgences to come, but they will lessen as the truth cements itself in my mind, which is still processing what's happened and been discovered, though to increasingly lesser degrees as each hurdle of acceptance is successfully negotiated.

There are bound to be times when things arise again as the realities sink in. These resurgences have not stopped the resurgence of me and you shouldn't let them stop the resurgence of you. You're stronger than you think and now you can recognise these 'blips' for what they are, you can allow them to run their course and fall away into the past, just like your abuser and the abuse.

Getting over mental abuse is a bumpy ride, especially in the first few months. One moment you can be smiling and the next in tears. Sometimes this is due to resurgence, at others it's concerned with the continuing process of the dust settling and your sight becoming clearer.

Things which you were holding on to, like fond memories or the hope that somehow you'll one day find your abuser changed and returning to you, have to be released in light of the realities, but this release can take time and a lot of pain. It's always painful to let go of the things your heart cherishes or longs for.

A prime example of how ongoing acceptance and release can make recovery a bumpy emotional experience occurred on Sunday 7th and Monday 8th May. On the Sunday, I found myself dancing around my lounge, which was something I hadn't done since Lissa had last visited me in Cornwall in August 2021. I was already in a good mood and was playing music. When a particular tune came on, I couldn't help but get up and start dancing, both cats jumping down from where they'd been resting and joining me out of curiosity. I smiled as I danced and afterwards laughed at the lightness I felt. During the rest of the afternoon I continued to chuckle and shake my head every now and then as I thought about what I'd done. That was a very good day, if not the best since visiting Lissa in Belfast early in January 2022, nearly a year and half before.

However, the following day was hard and made more so by lack of sleep. I was editing the impact chapters but struggling with looking back at the state I'd been in when Lissa's treatment of me declined, when I was at my mother's and in the first couple of months or so of living in Scotland. I was also struggling with the knowledge that it was down to her intentional words and actions. This helped lead to the realisation I discussed earlier in this chapter; that there were no good memories left from our time together.

Resurgence, bumpiness, acceptance and release; expect them and understand they're a normal part of the process. When it comes to the latter two, there's something you should know; they're also a sign of growing strength.

Chapter Fourteen

Stronger

Towards the end of March 2023, there were signs of growing strength. These were directly linked to acceptance and release. On the 25th, I took the engagement ring Lissa had given me from where it rested on the shelf in my bedroom. Less than a week later, on Friday 31st, I took down the picture of us as angels. They were stowed away and I managed to resist the temptation to put the picture back when it arose on a number of occasions in the days that followed.

Also removed from the shelf was the soft toy of Jiminy Cricket. Rather than being stowed away, he was placed on the bookshelves in the spare bedroom. He rests beside the volume of a book I wrote in 2021/22 which had both our names on the cover.

Around the same time, I also found the strength to remove her name from the cover of that book and the credit she was given as a contributor. The dedication within remains, as do the dedications to her that can be found in a number of my books. At the time they were heartfelt and, despite the urge to delete them, I'm staying true to my feelings at the time, just as I did when leaving a dedication to my ex-wife in an earlier release. I won't let the truth of how she felt detract from the wonder and beauty of my feelings at the time. She has already taken so much from those four years, but she can't ever take that from me.

These things were signs of growing strength. I was letting go rather than holding on. I was facing the truth. I was trying to remove the outward signs of my wish for her return. They reinforced this wish and were therefore unhelpful in regards moving on with my life. They hindered acceptance and the need to change my focus from her and us.

Even five months after we'd last had contact, I continued to miss her intensely. I used to feel foolish for this, barely dared mention the yearning I had to be with her again to my friends and family. When I'd expressed it before, there'd been disbelief considering how she'd treated me in the final months of our contact and the things I'd discovered relating to the majority of our time together. However, when I related this element to my therapist, she said it was hardly surprising considering she had been the main focus of my life for over four years, during which we'd had daily contact.

It was Lissa's presence I missed the most. I'd loved our life in Cornwall, savoured it and had never been so consistently happy before. Even in light of the knowledge she'd likely never loved me or genuinely appreciated our unconventional life, I still hankered after that time. This said, the emptiness and silence that had taken her place became increasingly bearable. Now, as I write this, the TV is commonly no longer on during the days and there have even been numerous evenings when I haven't played a DVD, happy with the silence.

This change began with a memorable pizza. It was mid-April and I took it into the lounge, resting the plate on my lap. Usually, I'd put on a DVD once I downed tools for the day and definitely when I was getting dinner ready so that I'd have some company while eating. This time, I chose not to. It wasn't forced, I was simply enjoying the peacefulness of a still and clear spring evening. Birdsong filtered into the house as I savoured the food and I found myself humming contentedly. Realising what I was doing and reminded of R2-D2 happily whistling to himself as he wandered through the desert in *Star Wars: Episode IV*, I chuckled and smiled. Things had changed. I'd grown stronger.

The fact I've gone from spending days on end lounging on the settee with the TV on, unable to do anything other than sleep, roll cigarettes, drink endless coffees and force myself to eat, to having a few days here and there when I struggle, shows I'm getting stronger. When I do have days like that, I don't blame myself and thereby undermine that strength. I accept and wait for the feelings to pass. In the meantime, I appreciate how far I've come from those days and weeks of stuckness.

Another sign of growing strength also occurred in mid-April. Somehow, Lissa had linked my phone to her EasyJet account on the relevant app. I hadn't severed this link, not out of wanting to keep tabs on her movements, but because it was a way to feel she was still in my life, that we were still entwined in some small sense.

I discovered she was flying from Belfast to Bristol on the 19th and returning early on the 24th. Though I eventually guessed it was probably in order to swap her winter clothes for spring and summer ones, something she'd done with the changes of the seasons when we'd lived together, I was initially taken by agitation and thoughts about why she was going to see her parents in Herefordshire. I wondered if she was going to come clean about us being a couple and engaged or if she was going to tell them about me publishing our story and claim it was all lies. I was essentially drawn back into thinking about her, the extrinsic focus rearing its head once again.

Knowing this was unhealthy and that, in truth, she shouldn't be part of my life anymore, I finally found the courage to delete the app from my phone on the 17th, two days prior to her flight. I rang and told my mother, who congratulated me after long having advised its deletion in order to help cut ties.

After I'd taken the necessary action, I felt stronger. However, it took a couple of days for the increase in thoughts of Lissa to decline again. I had to keep reminding myself that Now is about me, not her, that it doesn't matter what she's doing, thinking or saying in any other way than the potential damage she's causing other people. Thankfully, because of how far I've come, this reduced the focus on her back to the level it had been before finding out about the flights.

There were other things which changed in April too, but unlike deleting the app, they had changed without me having to do anything. The change just happened and was a sign of the healing that was taking place.

The first related to the habit of looking out at the drive to see if Lissa had arrived. I'd already noted its decline. It had gone from numerous times a day in January and February, to maybe only two or three times a day in March. However, towards the end of April, I realised I wasn't checking the driveway at all unless expecting a delivery. The habit and its associated feelings, both of paranoia and hope, had vanished.

The other thing which had changed dramatically related to the amount of time spent thinking about Lissa, our time together and what she'd done. As mentioned in Chapter Eight: *Stepping Stones*, I'd noticed the first time that I'd woken and not immediately thought of Lissa in mid-March. By late April, there were prolonged periods of not thinking about her. When thoughts did arise, they tended to be negative rather than positive or yearning. I'd often notice and tell myself to stop thinking about her, consciously changing my focus. This helped no end and I found my mood brightening as my attention continued to shift from her and the past to what I wanted to do with my life now and simple things like where I wanted to put new plants I was ordering for the back garden, which was quickly turning into a wildlife haven.

I have to say that the time of year was itself a great help. I was lucky that my recovery coincided with the recovery of nature from winter to spring. The latter has always been my favourite season and the fact its growing vitality echoed the same in me was like having the whole of the natural world on my side, chirping, buzzing and blooming with encouragement. When it comes to support as you heal, you can't do much better than that.

Here it's important to give a word of, not warning, but awareness; with growing strength comes the growing ability to face and accept hard truths. Things you may not have been able to see or fully accept before will become apparent because you're strong enough to move to the next stepping stone.

I mentioned the 1st May in the previous chapter and the acceptance that Lissa had conducted herself in full knowledge of what she was doing. The day after, I had a phone call with my father. It wasn't until an hour or so after it had finished that I realised I'd made no mention of Lissa. It was the first time since I'd met her that this had happened and it underlined my growing strength.

Not long after, I was finally able to see a truth which applied to the entire time Lissa had been in my life; right from the start, she'd played the role of victim. What's more, it'd been intentional. It creates attention in the form of sympathy and kindness. Moreover, in the context of a relationship, it puts the person playing the victim into the driver's seat, manipulating their partner into focussing on them. They become the centre of the relationship, able to generate attention whenever they like.

When it came to Lissa, she was prepared to use her mental and physical health, her close family, especially her parents, her employment, her interactions with other people and her sexuality to create attention and make herself my primary focus. Considering how much of this was created through lies and deceit, it was clearly purposeful and, along with her use of mixed messages, ended up creating my intense state of confusion during the final months and for a considerable time beyond the end of our contact.

It also served to create a kind of dependence after she moved out of the cottage in Cornwall. My focus was her, largely out of concern for her wellbeing thanks to her perpetual issues of one sort or another. When I didn't hear from her, I'd naturally worry. However, I'd never realised this had all been formed while we were living together, never before seen that she'd started to make herself the centre of my attention right from the start of our time as a couple.

Over the course of the two and a half years we'd lived together, she'd been highly manipulative and controlling in often subtle ways. Playing the victim in some form or another most days meant she created a lack of stability because there was little consistency. Creating this kind of insecurity is part of mixed messages and causes the victim to be on constant alert to the abuser's mood and needs, wanting desperately to bring about a prolonged state of calm.

Another element of mixed messages which she used intentionally was to promise me my dreams. For example, Lissa was well aware how much I wanted a child and that I've always felt I would have a girl. She knew my ex-wife and I had lost two babies due to ectopic pregnancies and she was likely my last chance to have children as she was in her mid-twenties and I was in my late-forties.

She purposefully encouraged the idea that she would be the mother of my children, creating a list of children's names on her phone and even telling me about a vision she'd had of our two children running ahead of us while we were walking through some woods in 2020. How do I know this was intentionally manipulative and not genuine? At the same time, she was telling her work colleagues I was the landlord she hated, had already dated one man there and would go on to see another for at least six months. Lissa had no intention of staying with me or having our children.

When Lissa was low or struggling with an issue or drama, I'd be supportive, nurturing and try to lift her mood. On the few occasions when the roles were reversed, more often than not, she would become low in turn, manipulating my focus back to her so I'd end up trying to support and lift her.

Her abusive behaviour was and is not exclusive to me. She also employs the role of victim with her parents and everyone else in her life. It gets her what she wants. She can more easily manipulate people. She receives sympathy, affection and other forms of attention, such as gifts. It makes people protective of her and willing to come to her 'rescue.' It's also a brilliant disguise, because no one would expect the most needy sheep of the flock to actually be a wolf.

All the above only became clear in April. It's what others had been telling me for some time, but it's often easier to see these things when you're not emotionally involved in the situation. The dust of all the confusion previously hid some of these hard truths. Those that were seen were barely believed and I tried to give Lissa the benefit of the doubt. Now I can see with much greater clarity because the emotional attachment to what I thought we'd shared has waned. It's also the case that many other stepping stones of acceptance had to be traversed before I could accept these things and release what I'd previously believed and hoped was true.

Ultimately, I had to be strong enough in order to face the truth about Lissa. I couldn't have accepted it at any other time, wasn't capable of admitting such a truth without completely collapsing. When it was finally accepted, I didn't shed a tear, just felt a deep sense of sadness and a strange kind of inevitability, as if I'd already known but had refused to consciously admit it. This is supported by how it came about.

I was sitting in the entrance to the greenhouse in late April having a smoke and coffee, watching the birds and looking at the wildflower seedlings I'd planted. I felt the familiar threat of tears, but didn't know why I was feeling that way. I asked myself, but had no answer. When the feeling arose again, I repeated my question and this time the answer came, the one which you've just read. I could see the entire time we'd been together in its true light for the first time. The truth had finally been accepted and showed I'd healed enough to be able to take that step.

You will heal too. As you get stronger, you'll be able to acknowledge things that once would have crushed the last of your spirit. It's as if there's a pressure gauge somewhere in our subconscious that keeps us protected when we're more fragile.

When I was clinging onto hopes of Lissa's return, that was self-protection. I couldn't have handled the truth that she had no wish to come back because she'd never felt what she'd claimed to feel for me or our life. When I was struggling with the clash of the persona she projects and the aggressive personality I'd discovered beyond, I couldn't have handled the truth that the latter is who she really is and she'd acted out of that self-serving nature the entire time. That would have had an impact on all my memories as well as on my perception of her, and I would have simply fallen apart, so I protected myself and what had been precious memories with the idea of a shadow-self. Only when I reached a place when I was ready, when I'd accepted other elements and had recovered from the initial impact of the trauma could I finally come to such a point. Therapy helped me reach it, as did all the words of friends and family during the course of many, many months, but it was me who had become strong enough.

I'd scaled the mountain and could see the truth spread out before me, and you will scale it too. There may be scary moments; your foot may slip and you may have to cling on while you compose yourself, cold winds may blow and buffet you, rain may lash at you, but you are making your way up, you are scaling it. What seemed an impossible climb before is being proven to be within your capabilities and, instead of waning, your strength is actually growing as you draw ever nearer the peak. Once you reach it, you'll likely find yourself stronger than ever before. I'll meet you there.

Chapter Fifteen

Happiness

Happiness returned in brief glimpses during March and April, like when I laughed after realising I'd smiled at myself in the mirror and when I danced in the lounge. These glimpses were also experienced in the garden, where I'd find myself smiling as I watched the birds coming to feed or saw wildflower seedlings beginning to rise, the reawakening of who I am encouraged by the reawakening of nature.

I was reconnecting with the part of me which gains so much from spending time surrounded by plants and wildlife, and which senses my connection to all life. This happiness was also because I was actively taking steps to re-establish the harmonious existence I'd had with the natural world when living in Cornwall. A sense of returning to the things you enjoy is a great way to feel lifted, as is a sense of achievement.

I was also becoming increasingly happy with myself and in my own company. I've always been happy with who I am on the inside but, when it comes to my looks, it's a different story. Lissa had purposefully targeted this lack of self-esteem in the last months of contact and so it was at an all-time low, one that had kept my head bowed in the local supermarket while staying at my mothers and had been a large part of my withdrawal once in Scotland.

I hadn't had my hair cut since shortly before leaving Cornwall, but was actually happy with the wild look, something I felt reflected my persona and love of nature. I grew a beard, keeping it relatively short, and this was also greeted with a nod. Part of the reason for liking both of these changes is because it meant I didn't look the same as I had when Lissa was in my life. I also genuinely liked how I looked and began to accept my facial appearance.

This is another form of acceptance; the acceptance of yourself. It's important, especially if your abuser targeted your weak points in regards your self-perception. You need to find a way to embrace yourself, whether that's a change of appearance, mindset or both. Maybe focus on points about yourself that you like, reinforcing that element of self-confidence and then moving out from there.

As the recovery continued, I reached a different place when it comes to my looks, somewhere I've not been before. Pardon my French, but fuck it! I'm going to embrace looking different in a world where so many want to look the same. It matches my non-conforming mentality and lifestyle, the latter including such things as no TV reception and no internet other than mobile data. I've got to own my difference and be who I am, and that's a wonderfully liberating realisation which brings newfound confidence and a smile.

Part of this liberation is from Lissa. She'd assumed control, taken ownership of how I view myself. Now I'm taking it back and it's time for you to take it back from your abuser too. Break the control. End their ownership of how you feel about yourself. Own it and never let it be taken out of your hands again. You can do it. They have no power over you anymore.

This sense of liberty was underscored by two memorable events in late April which revealed how far I'd come. The first was on Wednesday the 26th and there'd been a therapy session in the morning via Zoom. Afterwards, I felt more confident in myself and went to my neighbours to ask about a plumber, something I'd been meaning to do for weeks. I ended up having a lovely chat with them and returned home feeling pleased I'd had the courage and also holding a piece of paper with the number of a local plumber scribbled on it.

Deciding I'd done enough that day and feeling a little weary after the effort of human contact, I made a coffee, electing to ring the plumber late in the afternoon. However, before I'd finished the brew, I thought 'blow it! I'm going to ring him now.' As it happened, he was about to head past mine and so popped in within half an hour, seeing the problem and arranging to come by the following week.

After he'd gone, I put on the album *Urban Hymns* by The Verve. When the song *Lucky Man* came on, I ended up standing looking out at the Irish Sea through the front windows, hand to my heart as I wept with abandon. These weren't sad tears, but ones of immense gratitude. I was so grateful to still be alive, to not have taken my life due to her abuse, something which I'd thought of doing numerous times and had come close to on one occasion while we were still in contact. It was an overwhelming feeling of thankfulness and the lyrics 'happiness is just a change in me' really hit home, as did the line, 'I'm stood here naked, I smile, I feel no disgrace with who I am.'

On Sunday the 30th April I realised I was grateful for more than just my survival. I'd fed my last round of bread to the birds. It usually took them a day or two to eat all the pieces, but they were gone within a couple of hours. It was nesting season and so they likely had chicks to feed. It was also raining and so the bird feeder was clogged and, every time I cleared it, was soon re-clogged.

As soon as I saw they'd had all the bread, I changed out of my house slacks, slung on a pair of jeans and my trainers, and headed out to the car. Driving to the local store in the next village, I bought two loaves, which would ensure the birds and their chicks didn't go hungry. This was so me, my compassion for all life showing itself plain and clear, and that made me happy.

I got home and immediately broke up a round in the kitchen before heading out into the drizzle and scattering it, a pair of sparrows and a robin digging in without hesitation. Getting back into my comfy clothes, I made a coffee and, while I was drinking it, came to realise I was grateful for my liberty from Lissa. It was a HUGE step.

My gratitude that she was no longer in my life, coupled with disbelief in regards ever wanting to renew contact with someone capable of causing so much distress to another human being, showed I'd come a very long way. What's more, it hadn't taken as long as I thought it would.

I'd engaged with my pain. I'd explored my thoughts and feelings. I'd allowed myself to express the tears and torment. I'd written it down and talked it out. There had been no trying to avoid it. Instead, I'd faced it head on. By doing so, I'd dealt with so much that may have otherwise taken many more months or even years to surface, if it ever surfaced at all. I'd been honest with myself, my family and friends, and my therapist because that was the only way they were going to be able to understand and help. I'd been willing to be vulnerable, examining and opening myself up to the core of who I am. This had allowed the roots of the issues caused by the abuse to be discovered and, in turn, for them to be pulled out over time so the soil of my being was cleansed and the essence of who I am could flourish once more.

Don't hide from what's happened. Face it. Figure it out. Put the time into working through it. Own it and you will own your recovery. More than that, you'll regain ownership of yourself and your life.

That's what's happened with me and I've never felt so appreciative of who I am. Any doubt about what kind of man I am has been eliminated and replaced by firm conviction. I'm kind, thoughtful, gentle, nurturing and loving. Whereas Lissa saw these characteristics as weaknesses to be exploited, I know someone else will come into my life who'll see them as something to be cherished. They'll also relish the opportunity to share the unconventional life I live, one apparent in *The Gentle Man and the Butterfly* and well documented in *Field Notes from a Compassionate Life*. We'll share interests and inspire each other on every level. What's more, I know I'll trust enough to give them my heart when that time comes.

There's been a huge shift when compared with only a couple of months ago. This shift is that I've become open to the possibility of other relationships. There was a long period when I wouldn't and couldn't even entertain the idea of being with someone else. This was for two primary reasons. The first was that they wouldn't be Lissa. The second was that I didn't want to risk my heart again, believing it would be the end of me if it sustained anymore damage.

Looking back, I can hardly believe the place I've come to and am so glad this has happened as this book nears its end. Just over three months ago I was carrying a knife in my pocket, spending all day on the settee with TV series endlessly playing all day and night, going to the front windows to check the drive multiple times a day, becoming tense, agitated and anxious whenever the phone sounded, thinking about Lissa and what had happened every single waking moment, pining for her and hoping somehow she'd end up living with me in Scotland, crying regularly and still finding thoughts about leaving this life arising in response to the impossibility of dealing with all the confusion, pain and heartache she'd inflicted.

As I wrote that last paragraph I was shaking my head. It truly is unbelievable, and you will reach that point of looking back in disbelief too. More than that, you'll likely be made stronger by what's happened. I have been, not only in regards accepting who I am and how I look, but also because I know I'll never let someone else treat or torment me like that again. I deserve much better and so do you.

It was a lesson hard learnt, but it's often said that periods of struggle offer the greatest lessons because of what they reveal in you. If things are always good, you learn little about yourself. Hardship brings challenges and how you rise to meet them can tell you a lot about yourself and provide opportunities to learn and improve.

Seeing this process as a time of opportunity can help in itself. This change of perspective occurred in mid-May. Before that, I'd been focussed on the things I've already discussed, including the damage caused by the abuse. I then decided to focus on what I could learn from the experience. Instead of seeing the negatives, I started to see the positives, the silver linings. These included the increase in self-acceptance and the knowledge I'd know if anyone tried to use mixed messages to manipulate me in the future.

Shortly after this change of perspective, Caroline came all the way from western Cornwall to visit for a week. She was my first staying guest and we had a lovely time, which included beach combing, walking and spending lots of time chilling and chatting in the back garden. We also went to a nearby town famous for all its bookshops. Having a look around all those that were open, we went to a café for lunch and walked out of the small town to its tiny harbour on the Solway Firth, which is the third largest estuary in the UK. There was only a brief instant in the café when I became a little self-conscious, but the rest of the time I felt confident in my appearance and enjoyed our time at the town.

It was during Caroline's stay that I came to realise how much I love this house, adore the garden and enjoy living on the southwest coast of Scotland, at least for the time being. I think it was her appreciation of all three which helped bring me to this point. I even posted about it on Twitter because it felt so good to find those silver linings after leaving behind the only place I've ever felt I belonged.

On her last evening here, Caroline and I carried out a symbolic ritual. We all carry out rituals on a daily basis, like brushing our teeth, but they can be given far greater significance than purely the removal of plaque by combining them with symbolism. Symbols can be very powerful. Religions have known this for millennia. Countries and movements have also understood its power, which is why nations have flags and we're all familiar with such things as the swastika and CND sign. Even the business world knows how important symbolism is, just ask Ferrari, Audi, Ralph Lauren or Louis Vuitton. And this power can be utilised by each and every one of us.

In relation to Caroline and I, we both wrote three statements on small pieces of paper which represented elements we no longer wanted in our lives. Sitting on the veranda, we burnt each in turn and dropped the flaming pieces into a bowl. This may surprise you, but only one of the things I wrote down was directly related to Lissa, though all were indirectly connected to her. My phrases that I wanted to bring to an end were, 'I am ugly.' 'I want Lissa back in my life' and 'I will never find a soulmate.' As I burnt them, I imagined never thinking such things again. It was a good experience and the ashes were placed under a new plant I bought for the garden the following day, which itself symbolised the new growing from the old.

Caroline's visit was momentous in relation to the recovery process for one primary reason; it showed my journey of acceptance was done. For the first time in over two years Lissa, along with what she was doing and what she'd done, wasn't the focus of conversation. There was no longer anything to puzzle over. There was no more confusion or agitation. The extrinsic focus had all but come to an end. As result of these things, she was no longer central to my thoughts most of the time. Yes, she was mentioned regularly, but there were no tears and no angst. Some of these mentions were simply in response to what Caroline said, were part of normal conversation, such as when she said she wanted to visit the city of Bath and I told her about when Lissa had treated us to a couple of days there for my birthday in 2019.

Caroline's visit saw a marked difference in comparison with all the other times I'd interacted with people since Lissa had moved out of my Cornish cottage at the end of February 2021. By and large, I'd returned to being me and this return couldn't have come at a better time considering this book was nearing completion. What a wonderful confirmation of how far I'd come and a lovely piece of synchronicity.

The day after Caroline returned to Cornwall was Friday 19th May, two days before Lissa's 28th birthday and exactly a year after her mistreatment of me became quite blatant. It was the day of my last Zoom therapy session and shortly afterwards I was finally able to do something I'd been thinking of doing for a few weeks; I blocked and deleted Lissa's number from my phone.

It had initially been retained for three reasons; my hope she'd get in contact, because our Whatsapp feed contained many beautiful messages and due to my promise never to abandon her. The first of these dropped away once I accepted how Lissa had felt about me and her likely response to me publishing *The Gentle Man and the Butterfly*. The second only came to an end when I realised all the memories had lost their light and that what I'd shared with her hadn't been real other than in regards my feelings for her.

After those two reasons had gone, I regularly considered blocking her, but couldn't. I wasn't willing to break my promise to always be there for her and it wasn't until talking to my therapist that morning that this reason finally fell away. I came to see that Lissa didn't deserve the door to be left wide open. If she ever wanted to get in touch, she would have to make some effort.

More than that, my promise had been made without full knowledge of what she'd done. In fact, I still don't have full knowledge of what she did behind the scenes while in my life, but I know more than I did when contact ended and, in that light, it seemed reasonable that the promise no longer had to stand. I also felt lucky in a sense because her siblings and parents have no idea how she's treating them, her lies about them remaining hidden and all of them totally unaware of the things she's says about them in order to get attention. At least I'd become aware of her treatment of me and that was another silver lining.

Lissa deceives and manipulates everyone in her life, from family and partners, to friends and work colleagues. This meant I wasn't alone. Though I may have been the only one to be subjected to things like mixed messages and cruelty, she treated everyone with the same lack of regard. It would have been much harder to recover had I been the only victim and yet again I found another silver lining on the clouds that were clearing.

Blocking and deleting her number was the last action left to take. That's where I have to leave it now; with no apology or explanation from Lissa, no return of four small items she knew I wanted back and in the knowledge there's likely many other bad things she said and did which I'll never know. It's time to release the past and, with it, the pain of everything she inflicted.

There's nothing else left to do in order to remove her from my life and I've come to realise I didn't lose Lissa, she lost me. I would have stood by her side until my last breath, whether as a friend or partner. It's likely I know her better than anyone else and will for a long time to come. It may even be no one else ever knows her as well as I do.

There's still more healing to be done in order to lessen my thoughts of her, but that's going to be a longer process. All the acceptances have been reached, the path of stepping stones finally having bought me to a place where I've released so much and the sunlight now shining reveals our time together for what it really was.

It's a place of much greater happiness. There are still hard times and tough days, but after such sustained and severe abuse, that's not surprising. As you have hopefully seen through the process of reading this book, I was steadily gaining in strength and to have finally arrived at a point when I could block and delete her is a major achievement considering where I was only a few months ago.

This should provide you with greater confidence that healing and recovery do take place, even if it doesn't feel like it sometimes. Happiness does return, bringing smiles and laughter back into your life without the help of a single 'knock, knock' joke.

Find the silver linings, turn your back on the negatives and search instead for the positives. There will be some. You may have to find them in some unusual places, like me seeing Lissa's poor treatment of everyone in her life as a positive, but they are there. When you can start changing your perspective in this way, you open the door to greater strength, acceptance and happiness. You're no longer focussing on the darkness, but finding the sparks of light. They will bring ever greater brightness if you let them, if you hold them before you in order to guide you across the stepping stones.

One of the ways to do this is to think of what you're grateful for. Knowing you have things in your life to feel thankful about is an affirmation that there is some good left. It may be simple things like having a roof over your head, enough food to eat or clothes to keep you warm. It could be gratitude for friends or family. There are people in my life that I feel tremendous gratitude for and hopefully there are people in yours who are helping you get through the trauma.

Be thankful for everything that's keeping you going. See these things and know there are positive elements in your life despite what's happened. If you're a friend or family member of a victim, it can't hurt to gently point out things to be grateful for.

Feeling gratitude is a great way to bring positivity into a very negative situation. It's a way to find things to be happy for, including your chance to grow and learn from the experience. As I said, I've learnt how to recognise mixed messages and I've grown because I will never let anyone treat me less than I deserve again. This kind of personal development is a reason to be happy and there are many more. Look for them and you'll find them. Let silver linings and gratitude lead you back to happiness.

Chapter Sixteen

Looking Forward

So, here we are, we've reached the final chapter. I hope you feel we have a fellowship, that you know you're not alone. The ring we bear is the residue of the abuse. Once we wore it, were controlled and manipulated by its maker. When we first took it off, it still had the power to overthrow our senses; to confuse, frustrate and undermine the truth of who we are. That power dwindles in time, reducing to whispers of words and emotions.

It takes a journey and much hardship to cast it away, and even then the pain inflicted will sometimes make itself known through a fleeting memory, a song heard in a café or something said in a film or programme. The legacy of the abuse will leave its mark, but the biggest of these will be your return to yourself; stronger, wiser and with more self-belief. You will be different, changed, but many events in life change us.

Writing this book for you was relatively easy. I wrote down how I was feeling at or around the time when the things I've discussed were actually happening. It was part of my 'writing it down' recovery process. Editing the work, on the other hand, was hard at times. This is because I'm in such a different place now and it was difficult to read about the dark times and all the thoughts and feelings associated with them. I hope it has been worth it, that you have taken something from this book which will help, encourage or enlighten.

Not so long ago, I wished with all my heart I wasn't writing this, that Lissa and I were still together and the roar of my love was silencing her demons, as I once thought it did. That was a fantasy. Now I've faced the reality and am making the best of the situation by sharing my experience. Good is being drawn from the bad, and that's something worth celebrating. It's also something you can do. You can find the good in the bad, the light in the dark, and celebrate it, however small or seemingly insignificant it may be.

I can now see Lissa is someone who holds a mirror up to those she's with to make it appear like she's their perfect partner. I still miss her from time to time. She remains the love of my life, but she's also the biggest lesson of my life. I'd had the opportunity to learn this lesson twice before, both in relation to my ex-wife's departure and the only serious relationship between the end of my marriage and Lissa's arrival in my life. This lesson was that I needed to stand up for myself and not allow anyone to treat me poorly. Thanks to Lissa's treatment, I've finally learnt this lesson and have grown stronger.

I used to feel sorry for her. Now I also feel sorry for her current and future victims, and by this I don't just mean partners, but anyone in her life. She is an extremely calculating, highly manipulative pathological liar with limited empathy, no moral boundaries and little or no conscience, which makes her a danger to other people's wellbeing. I hope she never pushes someone far enough to take the step I thankfully never took.

The previous two paragraphs show a huge change in me. That's the one thing you can rely on in life; change. Hold onto that. Look back at the path of your life and see that every good period and every bad have been temporary. That's the nature of life; constant movement. Time is an uninterrupted flow from one moment to the next. It's a river that carries all of us and you can guarantee that the currents will change. They always have and always will.

There's something really simple that helped me see the truth of this. I was reading about the Taoist (pronounced 'Daoist') yin-yang sign. We usually think of it as motionless, but think of it turning instead. This movement represents the cycles of life. That's the true nature of existence. You could think of the light as summer and dark as winter. In summer is the seed of winter and in winter the seed of summer and the turning is the cycle that takes us from one to the other. That's how it is with our lives. In good times is the seed of bad and in bad times is the seed of good, even though we may not be aware of it.

Neither bad nor good times last. Make the most of the latter and know that the former will change. Sometimes the yin-yang may turn slowly, but be assured it is turning and transformation is taking place. You may even experience small good times within the bad, and therein lies the seed of what's to come. It may be meeting up with a dear friend, finding joy in blooming flowers or the sight of a butterfly. It may be taking a walk on a beautiful day, indulging in your favourite pastime, watching a new series or movie you enjoy. It doesn't matter what form the seeds of goodness take, they are there and they will grow. Every moment of your life is filled with a variety of possibilities and each has the power to germinate the next.

My life is still changing, the healing process ongoing. Acceptance has been achieved, but there is some releasing to do. The publication of this book will be a big step as I won't need to think about the situation or Lissa anymore, but can let it and her go. That is going to bring a tremendous sense of liberty and its one you'll feel in time because you'll reach the same threshold.

The hard realisations and the worst times are behind me. Now things soften and the healing will be gentle. My focus has changed and so will yours. Those stepping stones you've been traversing have been leading you down the road of recovery, even though it may not have felt like it at the time. Even the simplest changes will bring you greater strength, greater acceptance and a greater sense of returning to yourself.

Talking of change, I often hear or read the statement, 'be true to yourself.' Those of you who've been abused know this needs revising because our abusers, along with a great many unsavoury people throughout history, were being true to themselves. Maybe the statement should be changed to, 'be true to yourself unless you're harming others, in which case you need to get help and change.' Okay, so that's a bit clunky. How about, 'be true to yourself and the sanctity of others'? There, I think that's the one.

When thinking about the abuse, you could view it like a meteor strike. First you have the impact, along with the crater and the destruction it causes. Then, the dust starts to settle and things steadily become clearer. Life begins to return. Those green shoots hold a promise; that one day you will flourish again and only the remnants of the crater will remain.

I used to be very content in my own company before Lissa's arrival in my life. That contentment has returned for the most part. It has been said that loneliness is the pain of being alone and solitude is the joy of being alone. I felt a sense of solitude prior to Lissa, and that sense is now being felt to increasing degrees. This is aided by the knowledge that I am part of the whole, connected to everything. As Rumi stated, 'do not feel lonely, the entire universe is inside you.' Yes, I still have pangs of loneliness from time to time, but that's bound to happen after feeling so close to someone for so long.

I also used to want to be part of or start a community of likeminded people. One of the silver linings of everything that's happened is that I've come to realise how wonderful a community of two can be, whether as partners or close friends. This was underscored by Caroline's visit, when I savoured the likeminded and likehearted company.

I enjoy my privacy, but I also enjoy sharing this intimate space with someone of a similar nature. I'm remaining open as to what the future holds on this front. I'm not closing any doors, but leaving them firmly open in the knowledge I always have a choice as to whether I walk through them or not.

When it comes to my current location, there's a large, unfurnished and slightly dilapidated static caravan along one side of the back garden and I'm considering sprucing it up in order to make it available for people to come and stay, people who need time out, such as those who've suffered from mental abuse, or who are interested in nature and living in harmony with it, along with creative people who just need some quite time to finish a project. It would be a way of meeting new and interesting people. It could also become a plant nursery or art studio. Who knows, maybe I'll end up kitting it out with someone by my side, someone who has a passion for nature and movies, and senses the deep interconnectedness of all things.

The pairs of butterflies remain on my radiators, but they don't symbolise me and Lissa anymore, she never was a butterfly. They symbolise the hope someone will flit into my life and we'll dance together. As I said, symbols can be very potent and you can use them to reinforce your hopes. They can also remind you of how far you've come.

There's no telling what the future holds and you never know what's around the next bend. There is one thing of which I'm certain in relation to the possibility of having a new relationship; it won't be the abuse that gets to choose. I will choose whether or not I want to go down that road and am sure it will be a choice well made and for all the right reasons.

In the meantime, I'll continue to live in harmony with the rest of nature to the best of my abilities, savouring my interactions with the natural world. This will help the ongoing recovery process. The memories relating to Lissa have already lost a great deal of their potency and this will continue as the immediacy of her presence fades. At the same time, new opportunities will open up as the journey of life goes on.

After almost five years of being focussed on Lissa, over four years of abuse and more than two spent thinking about her virtually exclusively, I was mentally and emotionally exhausted. Now that exhaustion has lifted and it's time to move on. I'm glad to have shared my experience with you and hope it's helped in some way. For me, this is the moment to find release. I'm going to savour my newfound liberty and the rediscovery of myself.

It's time to start a new chapter which isn't part of this book or concerned with Lissa. It's a chapter filled with strength and the knowledge that how people treat me is a reflection of them. On the other hand, how I let them treat me is a reflection of me. I won't let anyone treat or torture me in such a way ever again. I won't even let myself treat me any less than I deserve. Whenever I'm negative about myself, I change my thinking, after all, self-worth starts with my own self-regard.

The clouds have all but cleared and I can feel the sun on my wings. May it shine on yours too and may the rest of your journey be free of wolves.

That's all there is for me to say, but there's one last thing for you to say. It doesn't matter if you're a victim of mental abuse, a friend or family member, or someone simply reading this book out of interest, I want you to join in and nod your head. Okay? Ready? Here goes, repeat after me; 'I *am* a beautiful human being.' Now, go out there and let your beauty shine because, you know, there really *is* life after mental abuse.

Publisher's Note: There is also now a fictional title by Edwin Page which relates to the abusive relationship and shows how our ability to love or lack of it defines us. Called *An Angel Comes Calling*, it is a stand alone story in which two contrasting timelines weave together, one with Lissa as she is and one as if she sought professional help. This novella is available in Kindle and paperback formats.

Appendix I

Selected Poems & Prose Written During the Journey

What follows is a small selection of poems written during the months since arriving in Scotland. They are presented chronologically and split by a short piece of allegorical prose. Not only do they provide examples of other ways of 'writing it down,' they also show clear movement in regards healing and recovery.

2nd February 2023

We are but fractions of stardust
In vastness unimaginable,
Each a glowing speck;
Faint suns in cold darkness.

For a time, I burnt all the brighter,
The fleck of my existence
Dancing with her in an eddy of time,
Both reflecting the other's light.

My illumination is now reduced
In her absence,
Floating aimless and alone
As the emptiness presses in.

* * *

Trapped in the past,
As if captured in one of the many photographs
Now etched upon my mind,
Its corridors a gallery
Through which I wander,
Viewing stilled smiles
Of moments gone,
Each framed in love and loss,
Each with me until the end,
So that, even though my happiness is gone,

I can see it was once real,
We were real,
Together.

* * *

I held my hand out to her,
She took hold,
But instead of drawing her from the darkness
I was drawn in.
Now, I see no light in my life,
Only in memories of her smile, her eyes, her laughter,
Her touch and my touch upon her skin.
Her company silenced my loneliness,
Her cruelty hidden in the shadows,
Now revealed and revealing a simple truth;
I remained alone,
The end of my isolation a mere illusion,
She; my kindred spirit,
Was no more than a ghost
Who haunts me still.

* * *

Love was answered with cruelty,
The best of what we can be
Answered by the worst;
Amused manipulation and enjoyment of abuse,
But love endured,
Its strength rising to meet her challenge,
Its arms continuing to embrace all she is,
In the hope of removing
The poison within her.

* * *

The wreckage of who I was
Drifted on the tide,
After being broken
On the rocks of her truth.

I am but the flotsam of her past,

152

Cast aside without apology, without thanks,
Left to the lonely depths,
Without a care
As to whether I drown in the misery
Of her purposeful creation.

* * *

Another tomorrow has become today,
Sleep the transformative divide,
By which I find release
From the repetition,
Each day rinsed by tears and repeated
The day after,
Day after,
After.

I fade away.

* * *

I crossed the event horizon
Of her heart;
The dark singularity
At the centre of her existence,
Drawing in all light
In the desire to light itself,
Only to find it extinguished
In the crushing black.

I crossed the event horizon
Of her heart,
And wept at sight of its emptiness.

* * *

The Broken Man

The warrior stood alone before the host, each a banshee bearing the likeness of her face. The sorceress remained aloof, high upon an escarpment overlooking the field of battle.

Day and night she summoned the banshees that cackled and howled, their cries filled with torments and untruths. They advanced with clubs, spears and blades, but he did not succumb. With every fatal drive and slice of his sword, the victim would perish with a vanishing scream, only to be replaced by another conjuration.

They tried to hold his approach, to push him back, but he would not be repelled. His heart was set on his goal and, though his progress across that vast field was tortuous, he would not leave the sorceress to her fate. He was set on his course, would rescue her from herself.

Bleeding from a thousand cuts and limbs battered by countless beatings, he would not concede defeat. With grim determination, he pushed on, gaze fixed upon her countenance, heart responding with the strength of feeling that kept him pushing on.

His blade flashed and sliced, the clash of weapons upon his shield like the chaotic peel of bells as the banshees tried to subdue him. Every step was leaden as his energy was slowly sapped by the relentlessness of his foe.

He caught the sound of distant voices woven into the chaos of battle, but remained focussed on his quest. It was all that mattered because she was all to him.

The sorceress brought forth more banshees with every dispatch, fearing her vulnerability without their presence. The closer he drew, the more monstrous each became, their screeches piercing, clawed feet pounding the ground. They cast cold shadows over him as they approached, larger, fouler, ever more intent upon halting his progress as she tried to bring ruin upon him.

His courage remained, but his strength was faltering, such was the ceaseless onslaught. His shield before him, a heart at its centre, he tried to push through, to break the cordon she had placed about herself.

His sword slashed and arced, the beasts falling and fading to nothing, only to be replaced by the next. Breathing heavy and stooped by the weariness of his body, he looked to the sorceress, the escarpment looming ahead.

Stabbing his blade into the ground, he reached his hand out to her. 'Take it! You can be free,' he called, the plea in his words echoed by his heart.

Seeing him disarmed, she shook her head and let out a rallying cry to the forces at her command.

The banshees were upon him. Discarding their weapons, they tore at him in feral attack.

He fell to the ground beneath their desperate assault. Trying to beat them off, he caught a glimpse of the sorceress as she smiled victoriously, amusement in her eyes.

The last of his strength vacated at the sight. There was nothing left with which to offer resistance. He had been fighting the battle out of love for her, slaying her demons in order to bring her liberty. It had seemed the noblest of causes, one to which he'd given everything, but she was without care.

Once, so long ago now, she'd cried out for him to save her. She'd reached out to him from her lonely hilltop. The forces amassed between them had seemed unintentional, the sorceress apparently unable to control herself and in need of rescue.

In time, he'd come to realise she'd always been in control, but it had been too late to turn back. Such was his love for her that there could be no retreat, only the hope she would be won over by his devotion to her salvation.

He knew she had conjured the banshees in order that he would be consumed by the fight, that his every attention was hers. Once it was, there was no escape. This was her true spell, and it was unbreakable.

He lay prone beneath the continued assault of the beasts bearing her face, filled with the chill of her gaze as his blood and tears mingled with the mud. His shield and armour were torn away and tossed aside. His clothes were made ragged and fell from his bruised and battered nakedness. He was no longer a warrior, but a broken man.

He looked up to the sorceress' high station, eyes pleading for her to call off the attack.

She turned and walked away, smile remaining as she vanished from sight, her voice carried to him as she called out for someone new to rescue, nourish and cherish her.

The banshees did not relent after her departure, but he could find no will to fight. He considered submitting his life to them as he lay in the darkness of their onslaught. They hid all light and the sorceress had stolen all hope in her wake.

Their claws delivered injury and infection. His mind was overthrown by thoughts of the sorceress and the impossibility of her true nature, one which had been so carefully hidden for so long. Flights of questions without answers circled and screeched, swooping to tear at the remains of the man he'd once been. His heart was poisoned by betrayal, clenching it tight and withering its vitality, his body left with barely the will to sustain itself.

Time lost meaning, was marked by pain and the howls of the banshees. The stamp of their feet and his continued tears turned the field of battle into a swamp of despair. He was drawn down into its thick darkness, which clung to him with the cold arms of inner death, its embrace threatening to snuff out the last of his light.

Unable to withstand more, knowing that either he succumb or force himself to rise, he reached deep within for some reserve that would see him to his feet. From a place with no name, there came the endurance to go on.

He pushed up against the weight upon him, the banshees still unrelenting. They plagued every move, clinging to his limbs, climbing upon his back; the burden of his past with the sorceress.

Wading through the swamp, every step was a labour of determination to be free of what she'd wrought upon him, though he understood he'd never be free of the sorceress herself. The true spell would remain for the rest of his life; the spell of love for her.

Slick with mud, he started to find occasional strength by which to fight. He wrenched his assailants from his body, throwing them into the gloom as his wounds slowly began to heal.

The discarded banshees would come leaping out of the dark, pouncing on him once again and resuming their assault. He'd stagger and sometimes fall, subdued by the incessant nature of her conjurings. Whether by the minute or the hour, each time he found the strength to repel them and continued on.

He found himself wandering in circles, filled with confusion as the mire gripped his feet, trying to bring him to a halt. Labouring onward, he was lost and consistently under attack. There was no destination in mind, only the drive to continue, to be free of the torment.

As the distance from the sorceress grew, the banshees appeared to weaken from time to time. A faint light began to dawn as he cast the beasts aside, the duration until their return increasing, giving him greater peace in which he found slow recovery.

The ground beneath his feet became more solid as the light continued to rise. He caught the occasional sound of birdsong, its lightness distracting his mind from the thoughts stirred by her banshees.

The voices which had once been distant became clearer. They were filled with care and concern. Containing their own magic, they conjured the faces of friends and family who encouraged him on, their expressions filled with love.

Continuing into the undefined, he found it taking shape about him, only revealing itself in the moments of his immediate passing. Without her, he felt alone despite the revelation of her adversarial truth. He had never felt such a bond of body, mind and soul, and yet she'd been his nemesis, this dissonance serving to confuse his mind and twist his heart.

The attacks of the banshees continued to become less frequent. At times they'd come silently creeping, at others they'd release fearful cries. On some occasions, he'd fend them off with relative ease, finding them faded and weakened by the ever growing light. On others, he'd be forced into temporary retreat and almost overcome by their vicious fury as dark clouds rushed in.

Their numbers slowly diminished, each skirmish won bringing him renewed confidence. Now that the sorceress had relinquished her control over them, now she conjured no more to replace the fallen, it was only a matter of continuing fortitude until they were nothing more than yesterday's pain and today's gentle sorrow.

In his heart, he would carry that sorrow for the rest of his days. It was wrapped in the folds of his love for her, would always whisper of her absence. Whatever land his steps were leading him to, it would be one without her. She wished no return, only to find new warriors to deceive and drain, manipulating their devotion with her enchantments until they could satisfy her no more and were discarded. Her story would repeat itself without conclusion, the sorceress never finding the fulfilment she sought, one which would only be found if she could but resist the temptation of the banshees' cries.

He sought solace as tears regularly arose from the sting of the wounds inflicted. He brought forth different memories from those stirred by the banshees. There had been times when they hadn't been present, when the sorceress had descended from the lofty position upon the escarpment. They had walked together in the field, which had been transformed by their togetherness, becoming a meadow filled with wildflowers and sunlight.

That had been enough for a time, but each occasion had been drawn to a close by the return of the creatures she feigned were beyond her control. The attention they brought fed a hunger deep within her that would never be satiated, would remain ravenous unless she could come to see the banshees weren't protecting her, but concealing her from the genuine love and affection of others.

As he continued through the strengthening light, he held on to the sunlit memories, for they were a gift. There was also another she'd given him, albeit without intention; the gift of a love so great as to surpass any he'd dreamt possible. It was the cause of his wounds, both deep and numerous. Without such feeling, there would have been no injury, but he would rather have been enriched by its presence than have lived without savouring its sense of completeness.

His bones began to mend, the voices of support continuing with their encouragement. The cuts were healing, though the deepest still lingered as sunlight broke over the distant horizon.

Its light was caught in his gaze. For the first time in recent memory, he wept tears of joy in response to the caress of gentle warmth, the chill within forced into retreat. In that caress, he found the first pleasure since last they'd walked through the meadow created by the enchantment of their togetherness.

Pausing in wonderment at what it was to be alive, he raised his face and closed his eyes to the golden clarity. He knew he'd be forever scarred and changed, but he smiled as he comprehended a profound truth which had been hidden for so long; a broken man could mend.

* * *

I want to sit with a tree,
Have it tell me of its life,
Of what it has seen in all its years.
I want to sit with a bird,
Listen as it sings me all it feels
And talks about life on the wing.
I want to sit with innocence,
For there is none in humanity anymore.

* * *

Spring blossom
Contains the essence of summer ripening,

Autumn fruitfulness and winter rest,
Of seasons now gone and those yet to come,
Change assured in these cycles of existence.

As it is in nature,
So it is in our lives.

* * *

In observational stillness
Rests an abundance of beauty,
Quieting my mind,
Wordlessly communing with my heart.

I find grace
By becoming lost in nature's detail,
Knowing I am part of its wonder.

* * *

My heart is a golden chalice
From which she drank deep,
Her own lost unto itself;
Unquenchable.

* * *

Emergence

From the pressing cold, I rise,
Casting off the shadow I had become
Within the murky depths,
Finding myself renewed
And opening to life.

* * *

The surface tension of my heart,
Waits to be broken by a gentle soul
Singing the same note as mine.

159

Two becoming one;
A harmonious melody,
Within nature's song.

The surface tension of my heart,
Is but the tension of time,
As I sing my note,
And wait to hear its reply.

* * *

Out of pain comes blossoming,
Out of suffering; hope,
Unseen in the darkness
Of inner turmoil,
Until revealed by growing light.

The bud of my mind opens to its light,
The flower of my heart blooms to its warmth,
Life is rich and renewed once more.

* * *

I am fallen to earth in flames,
Scorched by my journey,
A meteorite resting on a beach of pebbles,
Until careful eyes find me,
Gentle hands raise me,
A warm heart sees the truth.

The blackened shell crumbles,
I beat once more with the pulse of life and love.

* * *

In silence, you will hear it,
If you silence the voice within.

In simplicity, you will perceive it,
If you have the heart to see.

In your marrow, you will feel it,
If you are humble to the truth.

Rejoice and proclaim,
'I am one with all there is!'

* * *

31st May 2023

Red is the colour of my dreams,
Of all that screams inside,
Torn open,
To then be torn apart,
Heart betrayed with intent,
By the assassin within its halls.

Red is the colour she gave me,
But liberty bears gifts of its own;
Sun gold and leaf green,
Embracing all I am,
For I am home.

Appendix II

Suggested Reading:

I would strongly recommend reading *Narcissists Mixed Messages* whether or not you're a victim of mental abuse.

1. Begley, S. – *The Plastic Mind* (2009, Constable & Robinson Ltd.)
2. Birch, A. – *Boundaries After a Pathological Relationship* (2014, Amazon)
3. Dalai Lama & Cutler, Howard C. – *The Art of Happiness: A Handbook for Living* (1998, Hodder & Stoughton)
4. Hoff, B. – *The Tao of Pooh* (1989, Mandarin Paperbacks)
5. Simon, George K. Jr, Ph.D. – *In Sheep's Clothing: Understanding & Dealing with Manipulative People* (1996, A. J. Christopher & Co.)
6. Stines, Dr. S, LPCC – *Narcissists Mixed Messages* (2019, https://psychcentral.com/pro/recovery-expert/2019/04/narcissists-mixed-messages#1)
7. Stines, Dr. S, LPCC – *Victims of Emotional Abuse* (2016, https://psychcentral.com/pro/recovery-expert/2016/07/victims-of-emotional-abuse#1)

Suggested Listening:

Music, like movies, writing and artwork, can help lift your mood. Below is a small selection of songs with this in mind. However, not all are about how wonderful the world is because that's certainly not how I often felt. *Don't Give Up* is about holding on, *Move On* by Abba is about accepting that life is change and *Far Away* by The Levellers relates to things getting better

Then there's *Times Like These, Fuel My Fire* and *Shout*, all of which are songs which allow you to sing along loudly and let out your pent up emotions. You can even change the lyrics to suit you.

For example, the usual lyrics in *Shout* are 'these are the things I can do without' but, if you imagine you're talking to your abuser, you can change them to, 'shout, shout, let it all out, you are the one I can do without, come on, I'm talking to you, come on.'

There will be other songs which can help you let things out, cope and lift your mood, so why not make yourself a playlist for each of these? It really can help and I wish I'd discovered this earlier during the recovery process.

1. Abba – *Move On*
2. The Beatles – *Here Comes the Sun*
3. Bobby McFerrin – *Don't Worry, Be Happy*
4. Bob Marley – *Three Little Birds*
5. Depeche Mode – *Clean*
6. Donavon Frankenreiter – *Lovely Day*
7. Foo Fighters – *Times Like These*
8. George Michael – *Move On*
9. Gloria Gaynor – *I Will Survive*
10. Katrina & the Waves – *Walking on Sunshine*
11. The Levellers – *Far Away*
12. Louis Armstrong – *Wonderful World*
13. Nina Simone – *Feeling Good*
14. Peter Gabriel & Kate Bush – *Don't Give Up*
15. Prince – *Positivity*
16. The Prodigy – *Fuel My Fire*
17. Simon & Garfunkle – *Feeling Groovy*
18. Talk Talk – *Life's What You Make It*
19. Tears for Fears – *Shout*
20. The Verve – *This Time*

Appendix III

Useful Contacts

Have a look online and you'll find plenty of advice and help available for victims of mental/emotional abuse. There are many useful articles relating to various elements of abuse because it is not as rare as people may think.

Here are just a few sites of relevance. One bonus of the internet is that, wherever you are in the world, you can utilise these sites and also find others in your home country. Some provide information about abuse and others, like Mind, Relate and The Samaritans, also offer you the ability to talk to someone. Please take that opportunity if needed.

Abuse:
1. betterup.com
2. themendproject.com
3. mind.org.uk
4. ncdv.org.uk (National Centre for Domestic Violence)
5. relate.org.uk
6. samaritans.org
7. stoprelationshipabuse.org (The Centre for Relationship Abuse Awareness)
8. victimsupport.org

How to Contact Me

A couple of months after the publication of this book, I deactivated my Twitter account soon after it became known as X. It was having a negative impact on my self-confidence, self-worth and levels of anxiety. No longer engaging with social media has helped a great deal and I'd recommend it. This said, you can still find me on LinkedIn and Messenger. In both cases, my profile picture is a head and shoulders shot of me next to a silver birch tree.

Stay strong and know you're not alone.

Publisher's Note: Two further books are now available which relate to Mr Page's relationship with Miss O'Callaghan. The first is a short fiction entitled *An Angel Comes Calling: Of Heaven and Hell.* It features two contrasting timelines which weave together, one featuring Lissa as she is and one portraying an imagined version of her as if she sought professional help when embarking on her double life. It shows how our ability to love or lack of it defines us.

The second is a small volume of poetry that relates to the aftermath of the relationship. Entitled *Lost Souls: One lost to love, the other to itself,* the paperback and hardback editions include images accompanying the poems.